1   00   99   98   5   4   3   2   1

ry of Congress Cataloging-in-Publication Data

Richard E.
vanced wealth transfer under new tax laws: case studies simplify sophisti-
l strategies to reduce estate taxes/Richard E. Haas.
      cm.
ludes index.
N 1-56625-097-8
nheritance and transfer tax — Law and legislation — United States.
tate planning — United States. I. Title.
572.Z9H253 1998
305'3 — dc21   97-53281
                                                       CIP

s Books, Inc.
ast Illinois Street
go, Illinois 60611

d in the United States of America

Advanc[
Wealth Tr[
Under Ne[
Laws

Case Studies Si[
Sophisticated Strat[
Reduce Estate T[

Richard E. Ha[

Bonus Books, Inc., Chi[

This book is dedicated to my two wonderful children, Shaleece and Brent, who give meaning and purpose to my life. It is also dedicated to my clients, who have shown through their planning a great deal of love and concern for their children and the world in which they will live.

Contents

Introduction

Over the past several years I have worked with families who have built significant estates and do not want to see the fruits of their labor destroyed by taxes. Many members of the senior generation have expressed concerns about the affect that the inheritance they leave may have on their children. They do not want their children or grandchildren to lose the initiative to work hard, thinking that the inheritance is all they need. Recently, an additional concern has gained importance as well: fears of frivolous litigation. To address these concerns and help people attain their goals, I developed the concepts of Wealth Architecture® to assist in the design and illustration of plans to build a wall around family wealth. The Tax Relief Act of 1997 made planning all the more important because it provided more incentive by reducing capital gains taxes immediately, while phasing in limited increases in the amount that can be given before triggering estate or gift tax.

The tools of advanced wealth transfer planning are complex. *Real asset protection and "simplicity" are not compat-*

ible concepts. From an estate-planning standpoint, one can usually buy life insurance to pay taxes when due — a simple solution. Some insurance agents even advertise using slogans like "Reduce Your Estate Taxes by 90 Percent," while they do nothing to actually reduce the tax itself. However, few people are excited about the idea of paying tens of thousands of dollars per year in estate taxes, even at a discount. Consequently, they must use techniques that are more sophisticated if they really intend to reduce the estate tax burden. Many of the tools that work towards reducing taxes are also useful for protecting assets from litigation.

I decided to write this book to help professionals who advise families on sophisticated estate planning strategies better understand the alternatives, and so that they can help their clients understand these plans. People who do not understand a concept rarely implement it, unless they act from fear or faith that the advisor **knows** that it is best for them. Often the result is frustration or anger when the family discovers the *dis*advantages of the great-*sounding*, well-intentioned plan.

Most books written for the professional advisor leave a void, in that they are generally focused on a particular tool, like the charitable remainder trust, or they cover only the basic concepts. This book covers cutting-edge concepts, while remaining understandable to those who must design and communicate the plans, as well as to the clients who make the final planning decisions. It is heavily documented with appendices and endnotes to assist those professionals who may not be experts in the various techniques get an overview of the concepts. They will also be able to review the legal and financial details without having to look up the source material. For the reader who is more concerned about concept than documentation, the basic text has been kept relatively uncluttered by tax or mathematical details.

The book is organized around case studies that are loosely constructed around actual cases in which I have been involved. I felt it would be more helpful to see how the various tools work within the construct of real plans for real families. While every family's situation and objectives are different, the techniques used can apply to similar circumstances. The goal I have set out is to help the reader see the big picture, and how the various planning tools solve specific problems. The chapter text will be less technical in nature (as much as possible), with the more detailed information available in the appendices and endnotes.

A book like this cannot be completed without the work and input of many people. I owe a great deal to the numerous people who have taught me useful lessons over the years. I have learned a great deal from a number of top estate planning attorneys who have always been there to share ideas and answer questions. Special thanks go to attorneys Lynda Moerschbacher and Barbara Beck for their many hours of guidance over the years. I also want to thank my family, who put up with long stretches when I was unavailable because of the work I undertook to finish this project. Several clients were also instrumental in this endeavor as they encouraged me to share my thoughts with others. John Burgess, Eldon and Mariana Becker, Hans and Carmen Biland, Bob Bayuk, Ed Barlow, and many others provided inspiration, motivation, and review of the manuscript in process.

Special thanks are due to my friends, Dan Rice, Rich Baer, Frank McGehee, and Jay Steenhuysen, for the ideas they shared, the lessons they taught, and the drafts of this work they reviewed. Their technical expertise and simplified explanations provided me with a great deal of material. I also might have given up in the early stages had it not been for the prodding and encouragement of other friends. Barbara Leon of IBJ Schroder Bank read drafts and gave continued input and encouragement. Professor Paul Schervish of Boston College broadened my horizons regarding the potential uses of this book. Kelly Zuniga of Sacred Heart University and Wally Munro of The Actors' Fund of America helped me better understand their needs as gift planners. Finally, I want to thank my associate and friend, Lori Solari, for helping to maintain and increase our business while I was working on this book.

SECTION ONE
The Basics

1

Building A Foundation

In order to understand many of the advanced concepts that will follow, it is important to have a solid foundation in a few areas. An explanation of the technical terms and concepts that run throughout the following chapters will add to your comprehension as we move from case to case.

Social Capital

The foundational concept is that of *social capital*. It is generally defined as that part of your income and estate that the government has declared you cannot keep. If you do nothing, when you die the federal government will charge a tax of up to 55 percent on everything you own, wherever it is located (even if you have property in England, Italy, Hong Kong, etc.). This tax, called the estate tax, is a tax on your right to transfer property you *own* to whomever you choose. The Treasury then uses this money for the deemed needs of the society, be they defense, education, social programs, etc.; therefore, we call this tax social capital. When someone pays this tax, it results in government-directed social capital.

In the following chapters, we learn how to **choose to self-direct** social capital. You cannot take it with you, but you can control where it goes and who will direct it after you are gone. Very few people agree on how the government should redistribute capital. The different needs in society are hard to address through the political system. Self-directed social capital provides a way for each person to "vote" with his or her dollars for the needs he or she deems important.

Too often people are not aware of the ways in which social capital can be allocated. Some believe that at least part of their social capital should go to taxes to address the needs for which the government takes primary responsibility. Others feel that various nonprofit organizations will do a better job, or they simply want more input than is possible through the tax system. I feel that the choice should be a conscious one, regardless of what the family decides.

The Transfer Tax System

Before we discuss the tools that will protect you from the system, you need to understand how it works. The gift and estate tax sections were added to the Internal Revenue Code in 1916 as a way to prevent over-concentration of wealth in a few families. Until 1981 the tax rate for gifts was less than that imposed on transfers at death. They are now *unified*, and the same tax is assessed regardless of whether the transfer takes place during the donor's lifetime or at death. It is an *excise tax* on the right of the owner of property to transfer such property to someone else; it is not a tax paid by the recipient, but by the person transferring the

property. The tax is not a wealth tax, but a *transfer* tax.[1]
This difference plays an important role. The unified nature
of the transfer tax system also creates a number of planning
opportunities that we will better understand as we progress.

The transfer tax does not affect estates of less than
$625,000,[2] but once it kicks in it rapidly rises to rates that are
much higher than income taxes. It starts at 39 percent (increasing to 41 percent after 2006) and has marginal rates as high as
60 percent. If the tax is due because of death, with few exceptions it must be paid within nine months of the date of death.
The rates *(before* the unified credit, that protects the first portion, is applied) look like this:

Taxable Estate	Tentative Tax
$500,001 to $750,000	$155,000 plus 37% of excess over $500,000
$750,001 to $1,000,000	$284,300 plus 39% of excess over $750,000
$1,000,001 to $1,250,000	$345,800 plus 41% of excess over $1,000,000
$1,250,001 to $1,500,000	$443,800 plus 43% of excess over $1,250,000
$1,500,001 to $2,000,000	$555,800 plus 45% of excess over $1,500,000
$2,000,001 to $2,500,000	$780,800 plus 49% of excess over $2,000,000
$2,500,001 to $3,000,000	$1,025,800 plus 53% of excess over $2,500,000
$3,000,001 to $10,000,000	$1,290,800 plus 55% of excess over $3,000,000
$10,000,001 to $21,040,000	$5,140,800 plus **60%** of excess over $10,000,000

For over a decade we have been working within a system that allowed the first $600,000 of an individual's assets
to go to heirs without any gift or estate tax. Under the Tax
Relief Act of 1997, signed into law on August 5, 1997, the
unified credit (term changed to "applicable credit amount")
will be gradually increased to $345,800 from $192,800. This
is meant to shelter the first $1 million from tax. The phase-
in of the larger credit begins in 1998 and will be completed

in 2006. It is of little consequence until after 2003 because the exemption equivalent will have only risen $100,000 by that time. The tax savings through 2002 come from the states by way of a reduction in the state death tax credit. Given the determination of Congress to "balance the budget" by 2002, one can only wonder if this minimal benefit was kept low for that reason and if it might be eliminated if there are budget problems. Even by the time the full increase in the unified credit takes affect, its economic impact to mid-range estates is only a savings of $153,000. While this has a major impact on small to mid-sized estates, it is of limited use to the large estate-owner. The benefits of the unified credit and the low tax brackets are still phased out for taxable estates in excess of $10 million.

The transfer tax system can be confiscatory in larger estates. There are many alternatives in attempting to reduce the tax burden. In the overall design to build a wall around family wealth the foundation is the trust. Trusts have been around since early British common law. While the basic design of a trust is simple, the uses to which one can be put are almost endless. Although you may be very familiar with trusts, I thought it would be helpful to review them from definitional and conceptual perspectives.

What is a TRUST?

A trust is a legal document that has several essential components. It must have:

A *TRUSTEE* — a person or entity responsible for the ongoing operation of the trust according to its terms. The trustee is also the *fiduciary* who has the ultimate legal responsibility for the operation of the trust. As a fiduciary the trustee has many duties that can be traced back to the 1830 case of *Harvard College v Armory*, 26 Mass. (9 Pick).[3] Choosing the right trustee can be very important, as the selected person(s) or entity will not only be responsible for the investment of trust assets, but will also deal with beneficiaries and interpret provisions that may determine the timing and amount of distributions to a beneficiary. It is not unusual to see a trust that provides that income and/or principal shall be distributed to beneficiaries, as needed, *at the sole discretion of the trustee.*

Some advisors recommend the use of a corporate (usually a bank) trustee as the institution is set up to invest and administer trusts. While this may have its benefits, care must be taken to be sure that the corporate trustee will work well with the beneficiaries, and that the beneficiaries have some flexibility in replacing corporate trustees. In the chapters that follow, we will assume that either the grantor is the trustee or individuals selected by the grantor are the trustees. However, this is not meant to advocate one selection over another. This is a very personal, situational decision.

A *TRUSTOR, GRANTOR,*[4] *SETTLER, or DONOR* — the person who designs the trust and contributes assets to it. You will hear many references to the "grantor" of a trust. This reference to the creator of a trust who also transfers property is extremely important in estate planning. The grantor can be an individual or a corporation. We will focus on trusts established by individuals as a part of their estate planning.

A *CORPUS* — the assets in the trust. The corpus can consist of cash, marketable securities, personal property, real property, interests in a family enterprise, etc.

One or more *BENEFICIARIES* — those who receive income or other benefits from the trust. A beneficiary can have a current interest, an interest that is contingent upon other events, or be the recipient of the balance of the assets at the end of the trust term (a remainder interest). The beneficiaries can be individuals, corporations, or even other trusts.

Think of a trust as a big stew pot. The document itself is the pot. The trustor, grantor, or donor is the person (or persons) who chooses the type of pot, the recipe to be used, and the diners who will eat the stew. This person also puts in the ingredients. In the real world, the trustor is usually a member of the senior generation who is doing the planning. This is the person who is planning how best to transfer his or her wealth.

The corpus of the trust in our stew example is comprised of all the ingredients that will go into the pot, the meat and potatoes if you will. The *corpus*, or principal, is another word for the assets in the trust. The type of assets transferred will depend on the kind of trust and the purpose of the trust. Just as some foods do not go well together, there are assets that should not be put together in certain types of trusts.

Once the ingredients are put in the pot, someone needs to stir the mixture, check the flavor, add whatever is needed, and watch that the stew does not burn. The "chef" cooking the stew is the *trustee* of the trust. The trustee can be an individual, a bank, or a trust company. The trustee is legally responsible for assuring that the recipe is followed. The trustee can be given great latitude in the controlling document, or can be hamstrung and kept to very specific provisions. Trustees have a fiduciary responsibility to the beneficiaries. Such a duty requires the trustee to protect the assets, act with prudence (often expert prudence), and always put the needs of the beneficiaries first. You will see the importance of this later.

The trustee of a trust is much like a chef watching over the meal he is preparing and closely following the recipe.

The trustee is generally not responsible for determining whether or not the trust will do that which the grantor and the grantor's attorney set out to do. Most corporate trustees (banks and trust companies) only review the document to be sure they can administer the trust. No one should assume that because the trustee is an "institution" it has analyzed the trust to be certain it works from a tax or estate planning perspective. *Caveat emptor* is still the admonition of choice.

Finally, the people for whom the meal was designed and prepared — the *beneficiaries* — get to "eat the stew." They may be the grantors themselves, the heirs of the grantors, or the chosen charities of the donors — the people or entities about whom the creators of the trust are concerned. In the context of most of the planning we are talking about, the desire to provide for the beneficiaries creates the primary purpose for planning.

How Trusts Are Categorized

Revocable vs. Irrevocable

The first breakdown of trust categories has to be the most important: *revocable* versus **irrevocable**. To keep it very simple, you can amend or revoke (tear up) a revocable trust. If the trust does not seem to be working the way its creators wanted, they can essentially start over or get out of the arrangement altogether. An *ir*revocable trust cannot be revoked, and, with few exceptions, it cannot be amended. With an irrevocable trust one can have great flexibility, but that flexibility must be "built in" to the original trust. Minor changes can be made to some trusts, but for the most part they must remain the same for the entire term of the trust. As you will see, most of the trusts that have real tax planning benefit are irrevocable trusts, making the initial understanding and design of paramount importance.

Charitable

The charitable trusts used by families are usually "split-interest" trusts. The split is between the current *income* interest and the *remainder* interest. A charity (or charities) will get one part, while a non-charity will receive the other. Charitable trusts can be very effective tools for both estate and income tax planning. They also can be ideal for meeting charitable goals. The various kinds of charitable trusts used in advanced estate planning include the Charitable Remainder Unitrust (CRUT), the Charitable Remainder Annuity Trust (CRAT), the Charitable Lead Annuity Trust (CLAT), and the Charitable Lead Unitrust (CLUT). Most of these trusts will be covered in the chapters that follow, where they will be placed in the context of the most suitable situations.

Multi-Generational

Multi-generational trusts are used to benefit two or more generations younger than the creators of the trust. They are usually irrevocable. The most common, called a *generation-skipping trust* (GST), must be carefully coordinated with the estate plan, as there are severe tax costs associated with GSTs if the amount transferred is beyond $1 million per **donor**.[5] They are very useful for avoiding tax at the death of the "middle" generation when that generation also has a tax problem, and can create significant wealth to be passed down to two or more generations. GSTs can also be useful for insulation from litigation, and can reduce distributions should an heir decide it is easier to live off an inheritance than it is to work. They can also prevent assets from passing outside the family line (i.e. spouses).

A subset of the GST is the *dynasty trust*. It is meant to go on for many generations *without the payment of transfer taxes*, as opposed to the normal GST that simply skips to grandchildren. In order to go on for multiple generations, there are a number of special requirements that must be considered. This trust also has application for families who want to aggressively shelter wealth from creditors as well as from transfer taxes.[6]

What Trusts Do Not Accomplish

In recent years, some people have talked about a "special" trust that a friend set up with a company that helps people protect their assets. The story usually goes that the friend's regular lawyer "does not know" about this unique trust, as only a few of the wealthiest people have paid to research the issues and have this special document drafted. Supposedly, attorneys do not want us to know about it because once we set up such a trust we will never need them again. This author has been told that assets can be sold without capital gains tax, that the donors can deduct all expenses associated with owning their homes (like the gardener, water, electricity, etc.) because the trust has to keep up and maintain the assets, and the *coup de grace* — there are no gift or estate taxes.

Well, there are some top attorneys and **very** wealthy people who would **love** to use such a trust if it had any chance of working. It does not. Promoters of these "constitutional trusts" as they are sometimes called, attempt to say that because the constitution protects our right to contract, and a trust is a contract, we can have it do anything we want. Sorry. If the grantor retains an income interest in a trust, or retains a number of other powers during his or her lifetime, then leaving the trust assets to children or other heirs will result in estate taxes.[7]

Ownership Versus Control

Another concept that is important in building a foundation of knowledge is "ownership versus control." Most people like to "own" things, or so they think. However, with ownership comes liability, taxes, etc. Is it really more important to own something, or is control good enough? If you get to control assets and decide what to buy and sell, and when to do it, would that help? What if you receive the income in either event? What if you can take reasonable compensation for managing the assets? If you are willing to give up ownership, but retain control, you might be able to avoid capital gains and estate taxes. This may be sounding better.

People often can do more with money they control than money they own. There is only so much people can truly consume. Beyond that, wealth accumulates in the form of additional assets, only to have the government tax them away at death. The government encourages everyone to save money in retirement plans (pension, profit sharing, 401(k), and IRA), but if they are *too* successful taxes can consume up to 80 percent of retirement plan assets at death.[8]

Summary

Trusts are very important in the development of a sound family wealth-transfer plan. The proper design of trust documents, and the integration of the documents into the plan, can provide the strength and impenetrability of the wall that will protect family wealth. Combining various trusts and discounting techniques will allow the structure to meet the most unusual circumstances. This comprehensive planning will allow families to effectively make well thought out decisions on the direction of their social capital.

When families are considering trusts and other techniques to transfer their wealth from generation to generation, all members of the adult generations should be involved in the process. Advisors can help with the technical aspects of the plan, but it will all be for naught if the younger generations are not properly prepared to receive the money. All too often they are not trained in the management of large sums of money. Neither are they aware of how important it may be to the older generation to maintain a relatively modest lifestyle, even though larger sums are available. Children who are not emotionally and educationally prepared to receive large amounts of family wealth frequently lose much of what their parents worked hard for and diligently planned to pass on.

2

Protecting the Growing Estate

Many families have not yet reached the point where their assets and income are adequate for them to be concerned about the redirection of current wealth to family members or the community. These families have enough wealth that there is an important need to protect it, but this need is secondary to the living needs of the senior generation. For them, the basics need to be considered.

Let's look at the following family:

John Rocket is a forty-five-year-old aerospace engineer. His wife, Mary, is forty years old and a third grade teacher at the local public school. They have three children, ages seventeen, fifteen, and eleven. They have owned their home for sixteen years. It has a value of $375,000, with a mortgage of $125,000. They have been prudent investors for most of their married life and now have three rental properties with a net equity of $600,000. Last year Mary inherited a $300,000 art collection from her mother. In addition,

John has $300,000 in his 401(k) plan and Mary has $50,000 in an IRA. They have about $100,000 in mutual funds and bank accounts. There is $300,000 of group term insurance on John's life. The net estate adds up to $1.6 million, not including the life insurance on John's life.

They have not done any estate planning in the last ten years, and during that time their estate has grown by almost $700,000. They have a simple will, leaving everything to the surviving spouse. The will has a trust that comes into effect only if both spouses die before the youngest child reaches age twenty-one. After Mary's mother died they realized that they should do some planning, as they do not want to pay more in taxes than necessary.

What would the results be if John died this year and Mary lived another thirty years, with the estate growing four percent per year? Here are the numbers:

	Today	30 Years Later
Net Estate	$1,900,000	$6,162,500
Estate Taxes	$0	$2,404,000

There are a number of things that can improve the Rockets' situation.

The Revocable Living Trust

Over the past decade, the revocable living trust has been one of the most talked about tools of basic estate planning. Many people have promoted it as a near panacea, supposedly solving most estate planning problems. However, for many families it is just a starting point, the foundation of their plan. While its benefits are real, its limits are not well understood. Let's see what it can do for John and Mary.

John and Mary are still young, as is their family. If either spouse were to die soon, the survivor is likely to live another thirty years. The survivor's long life expectancy increases the benefits of using a trust to shelter the amount passed tax-free by the unified credit from being taxed at the survivor's death. But before getting into the economics of the trust we need to ask the question, "Why a *living* trust rather than a *testamentary* trust (one created under the terms of a will)? What is the difference?"

Probate

Much of the discussion concerning living trusts revolves around the avoidance of probate.[1] Each state controls its own probate process, which generally applies to decedents who were residents of, or who owned property in, that state at the time of their deaths. Probate is a court-supervised proceeding, the purpose of which is to see that the terms of a decedent's will are carried out, creditors are properly notified, and title to the assets is legally transferred. When a person dies, either *intestate* (without a will or trust), or with an existing will, his or her property becomes part of his or her *estate*. So, when John Rocket dies the court will control the "Estate of John Rocket" during the probate period. The person appointed to take charge and manage the estate during probate is called the *executor* (or executrix if a woman). When probate ends, the assets are transferred from the Estate of John Rocket to the Rocket Family Trust, or to Mary Rocket if John dies with a simple will.

Probate costs money. There are also court costs. Many states have laws that set probate fees for the executor and attorneys. These fees are calculated according to the gross value of the assets in the estate, not by the amount of work actually done. Probate is also a public process. The probated will becomes a matter of public record, although many people prefer to keep their affairs private. Also, because probate proceedings are supervised by the court, there can be delays in selling property or taking other action that could cause inconvenience or loss. While there are advantages to probate that go beyond the scope of this book, this author's experience suggests that for most people probate is best avoided.

Management

The benefits of a trust can be realized during a person's lifetime, as well as at the time of his or her death. If a trust does not come into being until after probate, it is obviously of no living benefit. With a revocable living trust John and Mary would normally be the trustees. If they were both incapacitated from accident or illness, the successor trustees could manage all the assets without having to get court permission, and if one of them were incapacitated, the other could be sole trustee. If John and Mary were to decide to spend two years in the Peace Corps in the Amazon, who would watch their money? With the living trust they could put the successor trustees in charge with a letter, usually a much simpler process than when no trust exists.

These are the primary reasons for using a living trust instead of a trust will. Now let's look at why having some kind of trust is so important for the Rockets.

The A-B-C Trust

Under their current plan the Rocket children will be burdened with $2,404,000 in estate taxes when the surviving parent dies (using the 4 percent growth assumption mentioned above). Through proper planning and the use of an A-B-C trust, they can gain significant savings. The part that saves taxes is the "B" trust. Some practitioners call it the *bypass* trust, while others refer to it as the *credit shelter* trust, and still others refer to it as the *family* trust. The amount that can be passed at the death of the first spouse, free of estate tax due to the applicable credit (currently $192,800),[2] will be transferred into this trust. If no taxable gifts were made during a person's lifetime, this trust can hold $600,000 or more in assets and totally bypass the estate tax at the death of both spouses, including any growth after the death of the first spouse.

The assets that go into this trust are for the benefit of the family, not the spouse. The surviving spouse may have the right to the income from the trust, but can only have limited right to trust corpus. Usually the right to invade principal is limited to that which is needed for "health, education, maintenance, and support." Such a limited right is called an *ascertainable standard*.[3] This limited withdrawal right does not constitute enough control of the asset to make it part of the taxable estate of the surviving spouse. So, if the trust is properly drafted, the value of the bypass trust will not be part of the survivor's estate. In the Rockets' case we said the survivor will live another thirty years. If $600,000 of growth assets were put in the B trust and grew at just over 7 percent per year (no taxes considered), the trust would be worth $4,800,000 at the death of the surviving spouse, all of which will go to the children free of estate taxes. A look at the table on the following page will illustrate the benefit of the bypass trust.

The "A" and "C" trusts save no taxes, but they will be deferred. The "A" trust is usually called the *survivor's* trust, and it is funded with the surviving spouse's half of the community property and any separate property owned by that spouse. The surviving spouse has the right to withdraw principal at any time from this trust. There are no limits as there are with the bypass trust, and as a result this trust is deemed the property of the surviving spouse and will be fully taxable at the time of the surviving spouse's death.

Years Until Second Death	Value of Bypass Trust at 5% Growth	Tax Savings of Trust at 5% Growth*	Value of Bypass Trust at 7% Growth	Tax Savings of Trust at 7% Growth*
Ten	$ 977,336	$ 488,668	$1,180,290	$ 590,145
Fifteen	$1,247,357	$ 623,678	$1,655,418	$ 827,709
Twenty	$1,591,979	$ 795,989	$2,321,810	$1,160,905
Thirty	$2,593,165	$1,296,582	$4,567,353	$2,283,676

*Taxes assumed at 50 percent

The remaining "C" trust (and remember, these are usually all in one document) is called a *QTIP* (Qualified Terminable Interest Property) trust.[4] The QTIP trust is used to defer taxes until the death of the surviving spouse, just like the survivor's trust. The difference is that the surviving spouse has only limited flexibility as to withdrawals and to whom to leave the corpus at death. This generally protects the children from having their inheritance left to a new spouse or family. The surviving spouse **must** receive all income from the QTIP trust, but has limited access to the principal. The QTIP trust cannot provide that the spouse's interest terminates in the event of remarriage, etc., because this type of provision will not allow the trust to qualify for the marital deduction as qualified terminable interest property. If it did not qualify, the assets designated to go to this trust would be taxed at the death of the first spouse. A QTIP trust may be appropriate when the assets of a couple in a community property state exceed $1.2 million, or when an individual's separate property exceeds the amount sheltered by the unified credit.

3

The Tao of Split Interests

The Taoists have always had a unique view of the world that gives us an interesting paradigm for understanding split interest trusts. They look at the unity of the world and the balance between what they call *yin* and *yang*. The whole is always balanced between the parts. While this philosophy of unity may be true, it contrasts greatly with our Western view of the world.

We focus on contrasts and comparisons. Our language and our society are filled with differences — tall and short, old and young, good and bad, now and then. Tall only has meaning when contrasted with short. One cannot comprehend good without understanding bad. Much of our approach to life is based on the boundaries that largely define our world. These thoughts may help us better understand the very difficult conceptual framework of "split interests."

The whole is made up of parts. If we own something together, it is mine and yours, perhaps equally, perhaps not. Under common law there is also a "now" and "then" contrast, known as an income interest (or life interest) and a remainder interest. Do not confuse the "income" with actual cash flow. It may mean that, but it generically refers to the current use of the assets, while the remainder is the corpus left after the current use. Like yin and yang, the income and remainder interests are intrinsic parts in all ownership arrangements, and are incredibly important tools in wealth transfer planning. By increasing one component we directly and proportionately decrease the other. Since we start with the whole — 100 percent — if we take 80 percent for the income interest, the remainder must be 20 percent.

In the development of plans for the reduction of estate taxes, one of the most important concepts to understand is the time value of money and its affect on the taxable value of items transferred. Many of the trusts we will discuss have an *income interest* and a *remainder interest*. They represent the present and future rights to the enjoyment of trust assets. The people or entities who benefit from these different interests receive such benefits at different times. Someone gets an income interest for a period of time, and then the remainder — the corpus itself — is distributed. How do we know the value of those interests today?

Let's say your best friend from out of state came to you and asked you to cash a check for $1,000. You know he is good for the money; therefore, you agree, and he writes the check while you go to your safe for the cash. You give him the money, but then notice he post-dated the check **twenty years.** Would you go through with the transaction anyway, knowing the check would still be good in twenty years? I doubt it. You see, if you give up the $1,000 (call it corpus) today, and get no interest for twenty years, what you get back is worth less than $1,000 in *today's dollars*. This is called a *present value discount*. The amount of the discount is dependent on the time before you receive the money and the assumed rate of return (interest). If you assume a 7 percent net return on your money for the twenty years, the $1,000 you will receive when you cash the check is only worth $258.42 today. That is the present value of the check. If you think of the check as something that you will give your children (or charity) in twenty years, then what you are *presently* giving is only $258, not $1,000. It is referred to as the present value of the future gift. You get to keep the money in the bank, receiving the assumed 7 percent interest until the date of the check. Therefore, the present value of your *income interest* is $741.58 (total value of $1,000 minus the remainder interest of $258.42).

Whenever you split the two component parts, you must calculate the value of each part. The primary factors are always time and the cost of money (interest) as we just discussed. But in estate planning, mortality also plays a part. Let's say you want to sell someone your favorite painting, but he cannot have it until you die. The purchaser of the remainder interest might pay you $15,000 today for the contractual right to own the $100,000 (today's value) painting when you die. If you die before the anticipated time, the buyer wins. If you live ten years more than expected, he really overpaid on a present value basis. In the transfer tax system life expectancy is calculated from government tables, and the interest element is factored in based on current interest rates.[1]

Split interest trusts are amongst the most important tools used to *significantly* reduce transfer taxes.[2] The more yin, the less yang. The more income for the grantor, the less theoretical corpus given to the heirs. It is *theoretical* because the calculation is made based on time and interest rates, totally independent of actual results. A $1 million Grantor Retained Annuity Trust (GRAT) that pays a sixty-year-old single donor 8 percent ($80,000) per year for fifteen years, might result in a calculated present value of the remainder of $390,000.[3] That would be considered the amount of the present gift to the children. However, if the assets grow at a rate in excess of the assumed rate, they will actually receive much more. It is important to remember that even if they get more than $1 million, the simple passage of time makes it worth less. The discount is for the implied "time value of money." Were they to have the money to invest over the fifteen years, it would be worth more than it will be after the grantor has taken out $80,000 per year.

The nice thing is that the grantors control who gets what when they design the trust. Sometimes the pie is split between the grantors and their heirs (GRATs and QPRTs). Many trusts split so the grantor gets the income and charity gets the remainder (CRTs). Others lead off with charity receiving the income, reducing the taxable remainder to the heirs (CLATs). The balance of yin and yang can be used to build a stronger wall around family wealth.

SECTION TWO
Partnering with Charity

4

When Charity Begins at Home

W e have all heard the cliché that "charity begins at home." For many families that is not a cliché, but an expression of the reality that they do not want to leave money to charity until their needs, and those of their heirs, have been met. This can best be accomplished by splitting the benefits between the donors and the charities in a formal trust agreement. In 1969, Congress decided to codify the rules for split interest trusts in which the trustor would commit to give the *remainder* to charity after keeping the income for life (or a fixed numbers of years not to exceed twenty). The *Charitable Remainder Trust* (CRT) was formalized in the Tax Reform Act of 1969 as §664 of the Internal Revenue Code. It defines two types of CRTs, the annuity trust and the unitrust.[1] In general, an annuity trust is one that pays a specific sum each period. The amount is fixed as a percentage of the value of the initial assets contributed to the trust. A unitrust will have a variable payment, with the amount payable changing as the value of the underlying assets rise and fall over time. The percentage amount that is paid to those who receive the income interest must not be less than 5 percent per year, nor more than that which will result in a calculated remainder to charity of 10 percent or more.

A CRT is an irrevocable "split-interest" trust. The income interest usually benefits individuals (although it can benefit partnerships or corporations for a term of years not to exceed twenty), while the remainder goes to charitable organizations, most often at the death of the individual income beneficiaries. The trust is tax exempt,[2] providing a number of planning opportunities that will be discussed later. One of the most frequently mentioned benefits is the ability of the donor to avoid capital gains taxes.[3] Beyond that, the uses of a CRT are not well understood. However, we have discovered many interesting ways in which the donors benefit and effectively control their social capital.

The Basic CRT

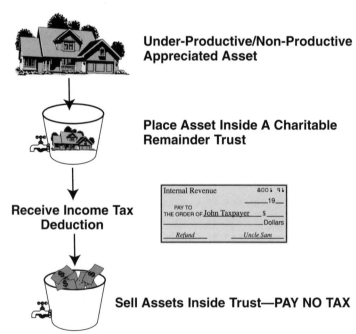

Under-Productive/Non-Productive Appreciated Asset

Place Asset Inside A Charitable Remainder Trust

Receive Income Tax Deduction

Sell Assets Inside Trust—PAY NO TAX

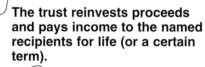

The trust reinvests proceeds and pays income to the named recipients for life (or a certain term).

At death of survivor or end of term, the trust terminates and the corpus is distributed to the named charitable beneficiaries.

Charity

A CRT can be very flexible, especially for an irrevocable trust. The donors can be the trustees without compromising the trust's tax-exempt status. They can hire and fire those who provide services to the trust, including money managers, administrators, special trustees, etc. When the donors name the charitable *remaindermen* (the charity or charities to receive the remaining assets at the death of the income beneficiaries), they can do so revocably. They can thereby add or delete nonprofits during their lifetimes. Most donors do not actually change the beneficiaries, but they appreciate the ability to do so. If a donor wants a nonprofit to absorb part or all of the costs involved in setting up and operating the trust, the nonprofit will reasonably expect that it be named irrevocably to receive most or all of the trust remainder.

There are other provisions of a CRT that also provide flexibility. For example, a married donor will usually establish a trust that provides an income for the life of the donor and his or her spouse. Given that divorce is a consideration, the income interest that passes to the spouse at the death of the donor can be revoked if so provided by the document. If the donor does not reserve this right, the "ex-spouse" would receive the income from the CRT after the death of the donor, *and* the donor's estate would be assessed transfer tax on the present value of the income interest. No marital deduction would be available, and the assets of the CRT could not be used to pay the tax.

There are other provisions that can be excluded from a charitable remainder trust document, thereby giving it even more flexibility. Most of them deal with the various rules that affect private foundations and can, but need not, affect CRTs. While the flexibility is not needed by most people, it cannot hurt to have a document that is as flexible as possible. Since the trust is irrevocable, the flexibility must be there from the start, or it cannot be there at all. This flexibility is most valuable in charitable remainder unitrusts.

The Charitable Remainder Unitrust (CRUT)

The unitrust is by far the most common form of charitable remainder trust. This is due to the fact that it can be designed to be more flexible than the annuity trust, it can be drafted to permit additional contributions, and it can have a higher payout rate and still qualify as a charitable remainder trust. In general terms, it is a fairly straightforward document that can have many "bells and whistles" added to it.

The first requirement of a CRUT is that the income recipients (usually, but not necessarily, the donors) receive an income of *not less than 5 percent* of the value of the assets per year. The trust is revalued, usually annually, and the payment is adjusted accordingly. If the trust value is $500,000 and the payout rate is 7 percent, the income recipients receive $35,000 for the year. The cash flow will likely be taxable (the details regarding the taxation of distributions under the four-tier accounting system can be found in Appendix A). The amount of income paid tracks the asset values. Therefore, if the trust corpus drops, so will the income. In general, it is considered prudent to set a payout rate lower than the assumed investment return of the trust. Any earnings in excess of the payout rate are retained in the trust, tax-free, resulting in the growth of the corpus and a corresponding increase in future income that will help offset inflation. There are situations where a higher payout rate may be in order, such as where older donors need higher immediate incomes, and have short life expectancies that would reduce concerns about long-term lower income from the trust.[4]

Some planned giving professionals focus on the payout rate and not on designing a trust that works for the donors and enables them to take the big step of setting up a CRT that will irrevocably go to charity. A number of years ago a client went to a planner with a primary desire to sell a fully depreciated apartment building that had also appreciated significantly in value. He was willing to consider a CRT only if he felt adequate provisions could be made for his family.* The final design for this seventy-four-year-old man and his seventy-three-year-old wife included a CRT with a payout rate of 12 percent.

Because he chose to name his college as the sole, irrevocable remainderman, the planner decided to disclose the deferred gift to the college's development office. The development officer was concerned about the high payout rate. The planner noted that even at very conservative invest-

---

*It is important to understand that the CRT provides for the remainder interest to go to charity, thereby effectively disinheriting the children, at least from the transferred assets. In general, donors who want to be certain that their children receive money to "replace" the donated assets will use life insurance to provide the desired economic benefit. The life insurance is often purchased by an irrevocable trust referred to as a "Wealth Replacement Trust."

ment calculations he estimated that the college will receive $750,000 at trust termination. The trust is irrevocable, as is the designation of the college as remainderman. The planner asked the college's planned giving officer if she would be pleased if a donor named the college in his will for a $750,000 bequest, to which she said she would be delighted. He then explained that this trust should leave as much or more, and had the advantage for the college of being irrevocable. All that was at issue was when the gift would mature and how much it would ultimately be. Through the CRT the planner was able to meet the needs of the donor and facilitate a major gift.

A donor receives a charitable income tax deduction when setting up a CRT for the actuarially calculated present value of the future charitable gift. That is the technical measure of the donor's charitable intent. In order to secure more gifts, all advisors should focus on the donor's needs. If the donor feels a need for a higher income than the institution is willing to provide, he or she will probably either not implement the trust, or will do so with another nonprofit organization.

Professional advisors, whether representing nonprofits or potential donors, should look at the plan as a whole to see what can work for both income and remainder interests. There are probably excellent legal and "political" reasons why a nonprofit may choose not to be trustee of a high payout rate trust. However, it seems that it would be in the best interest of all involved parties to meet the needs of the donor. After the client in the previous example felt his family was provided for, not only did he fund a substantial trust, but he has been working hard to grow the assets as he now wants to keep the assets intact for his college — a nice change of orientation from the start.

The charitable remaindermen receive the trust corpus at the termination of the income interest (usually at the death of the donors). Because the charity does not receive the assets until some future time, the charitable income tax deduction is limited to the *present value of the future gift*.[5]

The calculation takes into consideration the life expectancy of the income beneficiaries, the payout rate, and the current interest rates. Essentially, the younger the income beneficiaries and the higher the payout rate, the lower the charitable tax deduction.

Income Tax Deductions for a 7 Percent Payout Trust at Various Ages and 7520 Rates

	6.0% Rate	7.0% Rate	8.0% Rate	9.0% Rate
Age 75/70	$359,160	$361,220	$363,170	$365,130
Age 65/65	$254,060	$256,010	$257,850	$259,700
Age 60/55	$168,800	$170,470	$172,050	$173,640

This table illustrates the effect of various 7520 rates on the deductions for a 7 percent trust of $1 million.

In the Tax Relief Act of 1997, Congress adopted a new provision for CRTs. The short, general provision requires that in order to qualify as a charitable remainder trust, the present value of the gift to charity, as determined by the formula applying the section 7520 rates, must be at least 10 percent. This provision effectively bars young couples from establishing CRTs that would provide lifetime income benefits. It also affects higher payout rate trusts for those below about age sixty-five.

Income Tax Deductions at Various Ages and Payout Rates

	5.0% Payout	7.0% Payout	9.0% Payout	12.0% Payout
Age 75/70	$478,040	$362,400	$277,630	$189,980
Age 65/65	$372,200	$257,120	$180,410	$109,460
Age 60/55	$276,520	$171,430	$108,730	Fails
Age 50/45	$196,720	$107,740	Fails	Fails
Age 40/35	$114,000	Fails	Fails	Fails

Assumes a 7.6 percent discount rate (known as the 7520 rate) and a contribution of $1 million.

CRITICAL ISSUE: Even those with older trusts must be aware of this provision because it is not based on when a trust is established, but instead affects *contributions* to trusts after July 28, 1997. So a couple who set up a trust in 1994, and who add property to the trust in 1998, would be adversely affected.

If a new trust is established that fails the test, it is not considered a CRT, and all transactions of the trust are considered to be those of the grantor. Capital gains will be taxed to the grantor. The trust will be a taxable trust. In those situations where donors inadvertently make a new contribution to an existing trust, and such contribution fails the 10 percent test, the contribution is deemed to be to a taxable trust within the CRT, creating an administrative nightmare.

The statute provides for "reformation" of a disqualifying trust or contribution in order to qualify the trust. For new trusts that fail, it also provides that the donor can go to court (more legal tangles) and have the trust declared null and void *ab initio* — from inception. No one has yet addressed the issue of the charities that would be "disinherited" by such an action, and whether or not they could block such a voiding of the trust.

This new requirement eliminates the entire younger generation of entrepreneurs and successful investors from establishing trusts that would eventually provide significant funds to charity. The 10 percent test is measured by the 7520 rate, not market returns, so it has little to do with the real potential present value to the charities. Perhaps Congress hopes that these same individuals, foreclosed from this planning technique while they are young, will become more charitably inclined in their later years.

There are three types of CRUTs: standard, net income, and net income with makeup. The standard trust must pay the required payout each year, regardless of the actual earnings of the trust. If there are no earnings, trust principal must be distributed. Many nonprofit organizations resist using a standard trust where the assets are illiquid or where the income from the assets is inadequate to meet the required payout. However, so long as the donors are willing and able to periodically contribute additional cash to fund the required payouts, this is not necessarily a problem. If, however, in order to meet the required payment, a piece of an asset in the trust gets distributed out to the income beneficiaries a number of problems arise. First, fractional interests in illiquid assets are generally worth less than the pro-rata share of the asset itself. Perhaps 15 percent of the asset would have to be paid out to meet a 10 percent payout requirement. If the asset is highly appreciated relative to its tax basis (usually the case with CRTs), the distribution is considered a taxable sale by the trust. At that point the income recipients would be taxed on the gain from the paid-out portion, even though they could not reduce it to cash.[6]

The net income trust pays out the lesser of the stated payout rate or "net income" (usually just dividends, interest, etc.). If the payout rate is 7 percent, but the actual income earned is only 3 percent, the beneficiaries would only receive the three percent.[7] As will be shown later, the net income with makeup unitrust (NIMCRUT) can be very flexible. In its most basic form it pays out only the net income, but to the extent that the net income is less than the payout, a "makeup" account is created. In future years if "income"[8] is greater than the payout rate, it can be distributed, with the income in excess of the payout rate reducing the accumulated makeup (some practitioners refer to the makeup account as a "deficit" account). The following table shows how the NIMCRUT works.

Year	Trust Value	Payout Due	Income Earned	Income Distributed	Deficit Account
1	$100,000	$ 9,000	$ 3,000	$ 3,000	$ 6,000
2	$110,000	$ 9,900	$ 4,000	$ 4,000	$11,900
3	$120,000	$10,800	$12,000	$12,000	$10,700
4	$120,000	$10,800	$15,000	$15,000	$ 6,500
5	$150,000	$13,500	0	0	$20,000

This table assumes a 9 percent payout NIMCRUT. It ignores the "deficit account as liability" issue discussed in Private Letter Ruling (PLR) 9511007,[9] not to take a position on the controversial PLR, but for the purpose of simplicity in understanding this concept.

The Charitable Remainder Annuity Trust (CRAT)

This remainder trust is most suitable for older donors as it provides only a fixed income. Where the payment to the income recipients of the unitrust income varies each year according to the trust value each year, the annuity trust payout is fixed by the amount of the initial contribution to the trust. Also, there *cannot* be any contributions subsequent to the initial funding. This makes the CRAT quite inflexible compared to the CRUT. The annuity trust has an additional, complex requirement that it pass the "5 percent probability test."[10] Since the payout is fixed, regardless of earnings or trust principal, if the payout rate were set too high, it would be more likely that the trust corpus would be exhausted. If the mathematical probability of the trust principal being exhausted is greater than 5 percent, the trust fails to qualify. This means that high payout rate annuity trusts generally do not work, except with very old (eighty-five plus) income beneficiaries.

Maximum CRAT Payout Rates
at Various Ages and 7520 Rates

	6.0% Rate	7.0% Rate	8.6% Rate	9.4% Rate
Male 70	7.5%	8.4%	9.7%	10.4%
Female 85	10.5%	11.4%	12.5%	13.1%
M70/F70	7.2%	8.0%	9.0%	10.2%
M60/F55	6.6%	7.2%	8.6%	9.6%

This table illustrates that an annuity trust must have a payout rate approximately equal to the 7520 rate, except at older ages.

5

Uses of Charitable Remainder Trusts

The best way to understand the workings and uses of CRTs is to put them into the context of real-world situations. A CRT is nothing more or less than another tool in the inventory of the creative planner and builder. Standing alone it is a very simple instrument, but in the hands of a real craftsman it can almost create magical results. This chapter will help put the CRUT into perspective from a number of angles.

"Downsizing" a Home

In many instances, the single most valuable asset a family owns is its home. Many people over age seventy owned their homes for more than thirty years while they raised families, worked for one company, and felt no need to move to larger or "fancier" homes. In the San Francisco Bay Area and other locations with high housing costs, it is not unusual to talk with people who own homes worth over $700,000 that they bought more than thirty years ago for $50,000. Many of these couples have grown children living in other parts of the country. They neither need nor want the "big" house, and often would prefer to have the equity in the home available to provide additional income. While the new $500,000 per couple exclusion from capital gain is helpful for couples, there is still a big problem for individuals who divorced or were widowed a long time ago. Let's consider the case of Mary Bighouse.

> Mary is a seventy-year-old part time piano teacher who divorced over twenty years ago. She has three grown children and six grandchildren. She has a pension of $36,000 per year that will go on for the balance of her life. With all of her investment income, etc. her adjusted gross income is $90,000. Her net estate is $2.8 million, consisting of a 3500 square foot home valued at $800,000, a small apartment building worth approximately $900,000, and the balance in stocks, bonds, and savings. She lives comfortably, and after reviewing her estate plan some time ago, she started making gifts to her children of $10,000 each per year. Mary is getting tired of taking care of such a large house and would like to move to a smaller place in the country. She figures the new home would cost about $300,000. She has no debts. Her cost basis in the home is only $50,000, and she prefers not to pay more in taxes. She does care about a number of charities, but has never felt she could afford to make a major gift.

Downsizing the "Expensive Way"

Mary is going to move. She really wants to do what is best and she figures she will just have to pay the taxes and have less to spend. If she sells, here is what the transaction will look like:

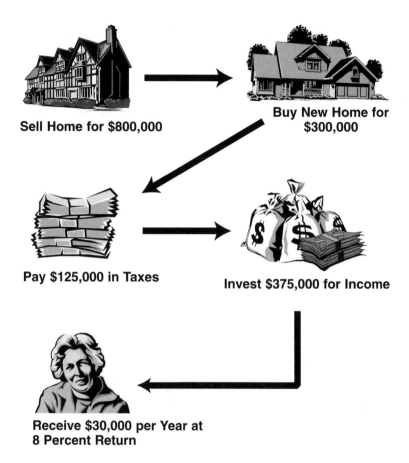

Sell Home for $800,000

Buy New Home for
$300,000

Pay $125,000 in Taxes

Invest $375,000 for Income

Receive $30,000 per Year at
8 Percent Return

Assuming the home sells for $800,000 net, there will be a taxable profit of $750,000. Under the Taxpayer Relief Act of 1997 (TRA '97) there is a $250,000 exclusion on the sale of a personal residence. That leaves her with $500,000 of net taxable gain. Between federal and state taxes she will pay an estimated $125,000. She will have a new home and $375,000 to invest. If the total return she is able to achieve is 8 percent, she will have $30,000 per year in additional gross income. When she dies her children will inherit $187,500 of the $375,000 after estate taxes are paid. That strikes her as just a bit expensive.

Downsizing the "Efficient Way"

Mary can reap significant rewards using a charitable remainder unitrust. In her case she wants $300,000 to buy the new home, with the rest available to provide income. With this in mind she decided to establish a 6 percent CRUT and contribute 50 percent of the house to the trust. The remaining 50 percent she will own as a co-tenant with the trust. When the property sells for $800,000, she will end up with one half of the proceeds, while the trust gets the balance. She will owe no tax as the net gain on the sale of half the house is only $125,000 ($400,000 minus $250,000 exclusion, minus $25,000 adjusted basis) and the tax deduction available from the CRUT is $195,352. She has the full $500,000 to invest, with $400,000 in the trust and $100,000 for personal investment. The difference is dramatic.

Sell Half
Outright

Contribute half to
CRUT and have
trustee sell

$800,000 Home

$300,000 Home

$100,000 Cash

PAY NO TAX

$400,000 CRUT

As you can see, there is significantly more money left to generate income for Mary's lifetime. When we look at the numbers, there is no question that this is the most efficient way to maximize the returns to the entire family, and to the community.

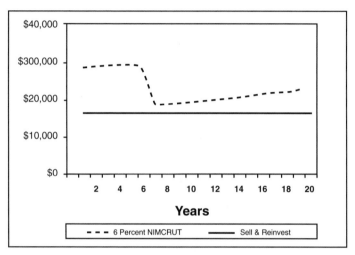

This graph assumes an 8 percent pre-tax return and a twenty-year life expectancy. The high cash flows in the early years reflect tax savings from the deductions.

Great care must be taken when dealing with a personal residence. Section 4941 of the Code imposes severe penalties for "self-dealing."[1] A donor cannot use trust property for personal use. Obviously, if Mary were to continue to live in the house after its transfer to the trust, she would be using trust assets, thereby committing an act of self-dealing. This can be a problem for some people, but there is usually a reasonable solution. In Mary's case she has adequate income to rent a place until her home sells. She even has adequate resources to buy a new home and make mortgage payments while the old house is on the market.

Sometimes people want to wait until they are comfortable the house will sell before they contribute it to a charitable trust. This alternative has extra risks. In order to avoid paying capital gains taxes the property must be sold by the trust, and not by the donors with the proceeds being assigned to the trust. This may not seem reasonable, but if the trustees of the trust do not decide if, when, and at what price they want to sell the property, all bets are off. It just does not work. What happens if Mary gets a surprise offer before the property is properly deeded to the trust? If she takes the offer, she will pay tax on all the profit. If she asks the buyers to wait while she gets her trust in place and the house transferred to the trust, she may lose the opportunity to sell at a good price. The bottom line here is that once Mary is sure she wants to sell, and is comfortable with the design of the CRUT, she should execute the trust and have a deed ready to record in favor of the trust. We usually recommend she get everything in place, move out, and transfer the property. People sleep better when they know the process is properly handled.

There are a number of issues that affect all CRTs funded with real property. We will assume that Mary intends to be the trustee of the trust during her lifetime. Under the law she is not considered an "independent" trustee, so special care is needed. Also, since real estate does not trade on a public market like stocks and bonds, additional requirements must be met.

Valuation Issues

When there is no readily ascertainable fair market value, there are two important issues regarding the proper valuation of the property gifted to the trust. One has to do with valuation for purposes of the charitable income tax deduction, while the other deals with the value for determining the amount on which the trust must pay income. They are separate and distinct values, determined by different individuals.[2]

Until the rules were tightened in 1984 there were many abuses of the charitable income tax deduction for gifts of art objects, real estate, and other assets that were not traded in a public marketplace. Before 1981, when the maximum tax bracket was 70 percent, there was significant economic benefit to high valuations for gifts to charity. To reduce the possibility of abuse, Congress changed the law to provide for the filing of a Form 8283 to substantiate the value of a gift of real estate or other "hard-to-value" asset when it is given to charity (this applies to charitable trusts as well) where the resulting deduction would be $5,000 or more.[3] The law requires an appraisal by a *qualified appraiser*. The appraiser must "hold himself or herself to the public as an appraiser who performs appraisals on a regular basis" (Reg §1.170A-13(c)(5)(i)(A)). The regulation goes on to point out that the appraiser must be qualified to appraise the property in question, and he or she must understand that an intentionally false or fraudulent overstatement of value can lead to significant penalties. The IRS has a big stick to keep people from taking excessive deductions.

This qualified appraisal cannot be done more than sixty days before the property is transferred, but it need not be completed before the house is contributed to the trust. However, it must be completed and filed with the personal tax return filed for the year of the gift. There are no exceptions to the requirement for this qualified appraisal, and ignoring the requirement will result in loss of the entire income tax charitable deduction otherwise allowable. Even if the house sells quickly, the sale price cannot be used for the calculation — the appraisal **must** be done.

When the donors are the trustees and hard-to-value assets are contributed to the trust there is a second valuation that must be done by an independent party. Remember that the CRUT pays the income beneficiaries based on the value of the assets in the trust. To avoid possible misuse of the trust assets, someone independent of the donors (usually designated a special trustee) must value the property for trust payout purposes. This is separate from the qualified appraisal, although the special trustee could refer to it if it has been completed. It is very informal, and usually a letter detailing the special trustee's opinion is adequate. It does not affect the income tax deduction. The new regulations proposed by the Treasury will negate the need for this second appraisal at the time of the contribution of the asset to the trust. However, an independent trustee (or an appraiser) must re-value these assets each year, usually on the first business day of the year, as long as such assets remain in the trust.

Timing of Sale

Mary would prefer to wait to transfer the property until she has an offer. She heard from a friend that she could put the property in the CRUT at any time before the close of escrow. Not so. An understanding of the issues will make it obvious why this does not work. There is a whole body of law that deals with the timing issue from several vantage points. The donor must avoid being considered the seller, assigning the income after the sale. The landmark case in this area is *Palmer v. Commissioner*, 62 T.C. 684 (1974). This is a very important case to understand for anyone involved in advising clients regarding the validity of a transfer of property to a CRUT at a time proximate to the sale of such property. To help you better understand the issues of *Palmer*, it has been excerpted and reprinted in Appendix B.

The CRUT is a separate entity. In order to avoid paying taxes outside the trust, the trust must be the owner at the time of the sale, and must have the absolute right to negotiate the terms of the sale. If Mary enters into a "binding contract" before transferring the house to the CRUT, she will have to personally recognize the gain. To make matters worse, the trust cannot distribute the cash to pay the taxes. The best approach is to deed the property to the trust before entertaining any offers.

There has been a great deal of discussion about this over the years. With real property, due to the Statute of Frauds, only a written contract can bind the parties. However, with businesses, etc., a simple oral contract could be considered just as binding, and may tie the hands of a trustee. If so, the transfer of these assets needs to be made well before any contract of sale is signed.

6

Selling an Underproductive Asset

Many people have assets that they have held for a long time and that are highly appreciated, but produce little income. Because they have an inherent dislike for taxes, especially capital gains, they avoid selling the property. Even since the passage of TRA '97, complete with its capital gains tax reduction, many people want to further reduce or eliminate the tax. People often ride a stock down from a significant profit to a real loss because they are unwilling to pay capital gains taxes. The incredible distaste for the tax sometimes drives foolish investment decisions. This does not benefit the owners or their families. An example of an actual case will illustrate the alternatives.

Anthony Wright is a sixty-eight-year-old retired realtor. His wife Linda is sixty and still somewhat active in the real estate business. He owns a large lot with an old, small rental house on it, the value of which is $900,000. It is his separate property and has an adjusted basis of only $50,000. His total net worth is $3 million and Linda's estate is approximately $1.5 million. They would like more income from the property, as it only produces about $36,000 per year in net operating income. There is no way to significantly increase the income from the property without taking on significant risk by developing it. They want to preserve as much of their estate as possible for their children so they have been hesitant to consider a charitable gift, but they feel their own income needs are paramount. They have completed most of their estate planning, and now they hope to find a way to increase their income so they can enjoy themselves and be able to make ongoing gifts to their children.

Selling the Expensive Way

Because their income needs are most important, Tony and Linda have concluded that they must sell the property. They are unwilling to take the economic risk of development and they do not want to trade for other property they would have to manage, so the only alternative would be an outright sale. The outright sale would allow them to save some tax by paying capital gains tax at the lower rate, rather than the ordinary income tax that would be paid if they subdivided and developed the property. Let's review the numbers.

The net proceeds from the sale are assumed to be $900,000. With the adjusted basis being $50,000, the capital gain will be $850,000. Applying a combined tax of 29 percent, the tax due will be $246,500, leaving them with $653,500 to invest. At 9 percent the gross income generated will be $58,815. That is a nice improvement over the current $36,000.

The Recalculated Capital Gains Tax

No one likes to pay taxes though, and the Wrights are no exception. Speaking of taxes, we just calculated the capital gains tax at $246,500. Is that the right number? Well, it depends on how you look at it. When people pay the tax, they do not just lose the amount of the check. They lose the income that could have been generated by that money for the rest of their lives. In Tony and Linda's case, if the total return they earn is just 9 percent, the "cost" of paying the tax becomes $22,185 per year times their joint life expectancy of at least twenty-five years, or $554,625! That is more than double the actual tax, and that is at only 9 percent. If they are able to generate a higher return, the lost income will be even higher. The income stream really has a "present value" equal to the tax actually paid, but people spend income each year and do not concern themselves with the esoteric concepts of present or future value. The bottom line is that voluntarily paying the capital gains tax (and it is voluntary) is the equivalent to giving away as much as 29 percent of the gain, with no present or future benefits.

Here is a chart that shows the long-term cost of paying the tax now, assuming different ages and rates of return:

Gross Cost Per $100,000 of Tax Paid

	8% Return	9% Return	10% Return	12% Return
Age 40	$360,000	$405,000	$450,000	$540,000
Age 50	$280,000	$315,000	$350,000	$420,000
Age 60	$200,000	$225,000	$250,000	$300,000
Age 70	$120,000	$135,000	$150,000	$180,000

Chart assumes death at age eighty-five in all cases and that total return is spent each year.

You can see that the younger people are, the more striking the difference. At age forty with a 12 percent total return, the income lost is more than five times the tax paid. People who want to control their money and generate higher income have good cause to want to avoid this tax, even at its lower rate. For people in high tax states like California and New York, it becomes very important because the federal capital gains tax is not necessarily reduced by state income taxes paid due to the alternative minimum tax. A large capital gain earned by a California taxpayer (or on California property) could result in a tax of 29.3 percent.

Selling The Efficient Way

The Wrights believed there must be a better way to sell their property. They considered an installment sale to spread the taxes, but did not want the risk of carrying the mortgage, nor did they like the prospect of a fixed income over a long period of time. They agreed to look at the benefits of using a CRUT as a way to control all of their capital during their lives and create self-directed social capital at the time of their deaths. With Linda being only sixty, and with longevity running in the family, the Wrights wanted to consider purchasing power over a thirty-year period.

As conservative investors they believe that they can earn a **total return** (dividends, interest, and capital appreciation) of 9 percent. They feel that inflation will stay in the 3 percent range over their life expectancies. After looking at the alternatives, they chose a payout rate from their CRUT of 3 percent less than their expected rate of return, or 6 percent. If they earn 9 percent over time and the trust pays them 6 percent of the changing value each year, their purchasing power will stay intact over time.

Let's look at the numbers (shown in endnote 1). Even though the projection shows returns in a straight line, two points need to be made. First, there is no way to accurately forecast future returns —there are no guarantees. Over shorter time horizons, investment returns can be negative, or minimal, or they can be quite high, as they were from 1982 to 1996. Second, the only thing about which we can be certain is that the actual performance will not occur in the smooth "no down years" manner shown, and with a CRUT the income will vary according to investment performance.

What have the Wrights accomplished? They have increased their incomes 52 percent, and they have avoided $246,500 in capital gains tax and $326,750 in estate taxes. Most importantly, the family also retains control of $1,746,000 in self-directed social capital at their death, exchanging taxes of $573,250 for the gift of over $1.7 million.[1] They have also generated a charitable income tax deduction of $219,000 that can be used to offset 30 percent of their adjusted gross income over a maximum of six years. While this technique maximizes income for the Wrights, it does not provide a benefit for their children. They can decide how much of their higher cash flow they want to allocate to providing more for their children.

This may sound like a great deal for the Wrights and their charities, but a bad deal for the Treasury. That really is not the case. The Wrights were hesitant to sell the property because they did not want to pay the taxes. Consequently, the income on which they were paying taxes was lower than it will be from the CRUT. That means the IRS will capture more income taxes over the next thirty years than it otherwise would. If the Wrights were to wait until the death of one spouse to sell, the property would receive a step-up in basis to the value at the date of death, thereby avoiding capital gains tax. Finally, if the Wrights chose to do so, they could still leave the money to charity at death, avoiding the estate tax. The CRUT assures that the money will go to charity, and the sale and reinvestment of the proceeds creates more current continuing cash flow for the Wrights *and* taxes for the Treasury.

7

The Diversification Dilemma

Over the past decade there has been a significant increase in the number of public companies. Many people who accepted lower compensation, while working long hours, were rewarded with stock early in the process, while the companies were still private. The successful public offering of the companies led many of these people to gain significant wealth, albeit in one company. Faith in the employers who made this wealth possible often leads people to maintain their stock position well after economic prudence dictates.

The dilemma is when to diversify, and how to control the tax costs. This is especially true where the employee is a long way from retirement and does not need income from the assets. Often the employee is earning ample income and does not want increased income that will simply add to taxable income. Let's examine a typical example:

Ed and Sue Henderson are a forty-five-year-old couple with two daughters, ages ten and eight. In the late

1980s Ed worked for a startup software company, Softco. He was employee number ten and was given the opportunity to buy 10,000 shares of Softco stock for $1,000. He was willing to take the risk, as he felt strongly about the company's prospects. Two years ago Softco went public and Ed's shares are now worth $2 million. In addition to the stock, Ed and Sue have a home valued at $450,000 with a $200,000 mortgage. Ed's 401(k) is worth $180,000, and they have outside investments of $500,000. Ed receives a salary and bonus of approximately $200,000 per year, and Sue keeps very busy as a homemaker and volunteer for two of her favorite charities. They are able to save money each year, and do not want more current income. Softco stock has performed well since its public offering, but Ed and Sue are concerned about the concentration of their wealth in any one company. However, they are also concerned that almost 30 percent of their gains would be wiped out by taxes on any stock they sell.

Prudence dictates diversification, even though Softco might outperform the market. However, capital gains tax tends to blind people,[1] unless they are highly concerned that the stock might collapse. Should they risk losing more than the tax by holding on and praying? Should they pay the tax and move on to a new portfolio? Alternatively, is there a more efficient way to handle the problem?

Diversifying the Expensive Way

Sue and Ed have decided they need to sell half of their Softco stock and diversify into a wider range of investments. They want to make sure they will have money available for their children's education. They want to be able to retire in twenty years, after the children have completed their education. They want to invest for growth for now, but feel it is important to periodically harvest gains as a way to manage risk. Based on their understanding of modern portfolio theory they feel they can achieve a 12 percent rate of return over the long haul, with the investments being primarily a diversified portfolio of domestic and foreign stocks.

Diversifying the Efficient Way

For people like Ed and Sue who do not need current income, there is a form of CRUT that provides a great alternative to a taxable sale. It is the Net Income with Makeup Charitable Remainder UniTrust (NIMCRUT). While this tool is very flexible and can work well for many situations, it is sorely misunderstood. Before we see how Ed and Sue could use a NIMCRUT, let's see how a NIMCRUT works.

As mentioned earlier, the NIMCRUT is one of the three types of unitrusts. The tax treatment is the same, with the charitable income tax deduction calculated in the same manner as for the other types of unitrusts. The difference is in what the income recipients receive and when they can receive it. NIMCRUTs are much more sensitive to investment decisions than the standard trust, so the trustees and the investment professionals involved with the trust need to understand the rules.

As its name implies, the payment is limited to *net income*. If the payout rate is 8 percent, but the net income received by the trust is only 3 percent, the beneficiaries will receive just the 3 percent net income. However, the "M" in NIMCRUT deals with the makeup provision. Simply stated, if the income actually paid to the beneficiaries in a year is less than the stated payout rate (8 percent in our example), a bookkeeping entry is made that gives the income recipients an opportunity to "makeup" the shortfall in a future year *if there is excess income* in such year. In other words, if the trust earns a 10 percent income in a future year, the excess 2 percent can be paid, reducing the cumulative makeup account.

Practitioners often refer to the makeup account as a "deficit" account, or even an "IOU" account. But these terms are misleading. There is no true liability. It is contingent because the excess amounts paid can come only if and when there is excess net income. If it is not earned, it is not paid. Think of it as a "withdrawal rights reservoir." The reservoir will rise as the income recipient receives less than the stated payout rate in any year, and fall as excess income is paid in other years. The right to pull something from the reservoir is always dependent on the trust actually receiving the income. The following examples should help make this more understandable.

Example 1

Year	Value*	Stated Payout**	Net Income	Actual Payout	Annual "IOU"	CUM "IOU"
1	$100,000	$10,000	$ 4,000	$ 4,000	$6,000	$ 6,000
2	100,000	10,000	6,000	6,000	4,000	10,000
3	100,000	10,000	14,000	14,000	(4,000)	6,000
4	100,000	10,000	10,000	10,000	0	6,000
5	100,000	10,000	8,000	8,000	2,000	8,000

*10 percent payout rate assumed
**Only CDs purchased, so no fluctuation in market price.

Example 2

Year	Value	Stated Payout*	Net Income	Actual Payout	Annual "IOU"	CUM "IOU"
1	$100,000	$8,000	$8,000	$8,000	0	0
2**	80,000	6,400	8,000	6,400	0	0
3	120,000	9,600	8,000	8,000	1,600	1,600

*8 percent payout rate assumed

**If bonds were held and interest rates rose, the value of the bonds would decrease as would the payout.

What is "Net Income?"

Without drowning you in detail about how this aspect of the NIMCRUT works, I need to differentiate between the definitions of income for tax purposes and for trust purposes. When stock is sold by a trust, including a charitable trust, it may realize a gain that will add to its "taxable" income. It can even have a taxable income without having any real cash to show for it. The fact that it is tax exempt simply means that the trust itself will not owe any tax.

Net income available to be distributed to income recipients is very different. A NIMCRUT can only distribute trust, or *fiduciary income*. The goal is to have income only on receipt of cash. Even if there is a "profit," it is not distributable to the income recipients unless there is cash that comes from the transaction. The rules are complicated, and for the most part they are set out in the Revised Uniform Principal and Income Act that has been adopted by all but a handful of states. A few states have passed legislation that specifically supports the idea that there is no trust income until the trust has received *cash* from the subject investment. Income *can* be defined to include gain on the sale of trust assets. However, most trusts I have seen do not define such gains as income, instead they add them to trust principal.[2]

If Ed and Sue transferred $1 million of their Softco stock to NIMCRUTs (one for each of them*), sold it, and invested in a portfolio of non-dividend-paying growth stocks, the trusts would not have any net income to distribute to Ed and Sue. No current income. No taxable income. Just an addition to their withdrawal rights reservoirs. The trust assets would grow tax-free, even if they periodically sold stocks at a profit, as there still would not be any net income to distribute. When they want income, they would have to convert the portfolio from being primarily growth-oriented to one with an income orientation. However, in a low-interest rate environment, they would never be able to draw down the accumulated withdrawal rights.

A Workable Solution

Remember, the Hendersons do not want income now, but they want to be able to withdraw it if they need it for the education of their children and for retirement. They do not want to suffer later if interest rates are low, so they need a way to tap more of their withdrawal rights reservoir. The solution is to use investments that create "income" only when desired.[3]

Several states have revised their principal and income acts to say, "you only have income when you have cash from an investment." The legalese is not as shown, but that is the essence of their laws. Let's say the trustees of the NIMCRUT invest in a variable annuity with XYZ Life

---

*The reason for using two trusts in this scenario is to get around the problems created by the new tax law. In order for a two-life trust to pass the new 10 percent rule, the maximum payout rate they could have would be 6.39 percent. With each setting up a single life trust, they can use a 9.3 percent payout. They can each buy inexpensive term insurance on each other to provide extra-tax-free money to replace the income lost at the death of either spouse.

(only life insurance companies issue annuities). They direct that the money go to the stock subaccounts (similar to mutual funds) in the annuity contract. Dividends are not paid out of an annuity in cash; instead, they increase the value of each unit in the fund. Even if they switch the investment in the annuity from stocks to bonds or money market funds, no cash is received until a withdrawal is made. That creates cash in the trust that would be defined as "income." Then Sue and Ed will receive a distribution. Such a distribution must not jeopardize the rights of the charity. In addition, the distribution can only be for the lesser of the accumulated withdrawal rights or the "profit" in the investment.[4]

The following graph shows what the possibilities of using a 9.3 percent payout NIMCRUT are, and how much "could" be withdrawn from time to time. The investment results *assume* a level 12 percent return. While returns of the past twenty years have been well in excess of that, the returns will not be uniform, and may or may not equal 12 percent.

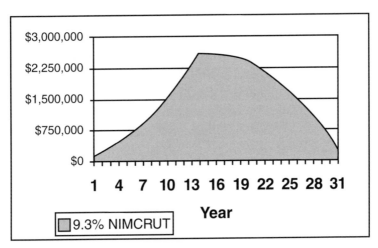

Potential withdrawals available from
NIMCRUT

If we assume that the investment returns 12 percent every year, how would Sue and Ed do relative to their objectives? How would their charities fare? First, let's look at the money they would have available to pay educational costs starting in ten years. The accumulated deficit would be $1,451,000 and there would be enough investment gain to easily allow them to withdraw money each year for education costs.

After educational expenses are behind them, Sue and Ed would be unlikely to need supplemental income from the trust. If the returns on the NIMCRUT investments continue at the same level, let's see what Sue and Ed can withdraw between ages sixty-five and eighty-five. At their life expectancy the combined trusts are projected to be valued at $3,255,000, resulting in a significant charitable contribution. As mentioned earlier, they must deal with the risk that one of them might die prematurely, cutting income in half. However, the additional cash flow created by having the higher payout is more than enough to pay premiums on a thirty year level term policy for each of them. The table on the following page provides a comparison of benefits.

You might remember that the charitable income tax deduction that donors receive for contributions to CRTs is the present value of the future gift, and for Sue and Ed it is only 10 percent. Some practitioners suggest that where the deduction is small, or unneeded, the trust should run for the lives of the donors **and** their children.

Comparison of Benefits
Ed and Sue Henderson

A. Input Assumptions:

	NIMCRUT	Sell and Reinvest
Type of Technique		
Time Period Projected	1998-2034	1998-2029
Income Payout Rate	9.30%	Variable
Income is Paid	Quarterly	Quarterly
Investment Period Measured by	1 Life*	1 Life*

B. Contributions:

	NIMCRUT	Sell and Reinvest
Fair Market Value of Property	$1,000,000	$1,000,000
Income Tax Deduction Permitted	$101,190	$0
Capital Gains Tax on Sale	$0	$269,865

C. Cash Flow:

	NIMCRUT	Sell and Reinvest
Income During Life (after taxes)	$5,895,330	$3,399,130
(–) Premiums Paid from Income	$96,000	$0
(=) Net Spendable Income	$5,799,330	$3,399,130

D. Estate for Heirs:

	NIMCRUT	Sell and Reinvest
Gross Value of Estate	$0	$1,475,065
(+) Life Insurance Death Benefit	$1,000,000	$0
(–) Estate Taxes	$0	$737,532
(=) Net Estate for Children	$1,000,000	$737,532

E. Benefit Summary:

	NIMCRUT	Sell and Reinvest
Net Income + Net to Children	$6,799,330	$4,136,662
(+) Endowment to Charity	$3,254,848	$0
(=) Total Benefit	$10,054,178	$4,136,662

*For ease of illustration it is assumed that each has a one life trust invested alike, and that death occurs in the same year for both. The children's benefit comes from $1 million survivorship life insurance.

The Two Generation CRT

Aside from the ethical issue of having the charities wait an extra thirty to forty years for the remainder interest, there are some practical and tax problems with the two generation trust, unless the second generation is already quite old. I first mention the ethical issue because I believe that overly "creative" use of the tax code is seen by many as abuse. When there is enough abuse to gain media and congressional attention, the response has usually been to destroy a tool that has the potential to benefit everyone — killing the patient to assure the cancer does not spread. In this case, pragmatic planning should rule out the two generation CRT.

For younger couples like Ed and Sue, we need not even consider this anymore, as the 10 percent minimum charitable remainder imposed by TRA '97 would rule out a two generation CRT for them. Only where the senior generation is very old would this work. In most cases the children will have to be in their fifties or older *at the time the trust is established,* or the trust will fail to qualify from inception.

This is a costly, impractical solution to assuring the children receive benefits, usually by those who are not charitably inclined, and who are also opposed to life insurance as an asset replacement alternative. Since Sue and Ed cannot use a two generation trust, let's see how a wealth replacement trust would work for them.

They want to be sure there is insurance to replace the value that would otherwise go to the children. If they were to buy $1 million of coverage on Ed, the average cost would be $16,000 per year for twelve years. The same benefit placed on Sue would cost about $13,000 per year. Survivorship life insurance is most cost effective. A $1 million policy that pays on the death of the survivor costs less than $8,000, a savings of 50 percent over just insuring Ed (these rates, all from the same competitive company, are the rates for healthy non-smokers. Smokers, older couples, and those with health problems will pay higher rates).

The Henderson children are young and cannot own the policy on their parents. If Sue and Ed owned the policy themselves, it would be taxable as part of their estate (bad idea). Therefore, they choose to use an irrevocable life insurance trust. Someone other than Sue or Ed must be the trustee, because if either insured can control any of the contractual provisions of the life insurance policy, it will be includable in his or her estate under IRC §2042. The trustee of this irrevocable trust applies for the life insurance on Sue and Ed. The fully guaranteed annual premium for a typical survivorship whole life is $8,000 at their age. There are myriad choices of insurance contracts that could work, but for this purpose, and at their age, this is a good example.

With an irrevocable life insurance trust funded by a survivorship policy, the Hendersons are able to see that their children get a significant asset to replace the wealth that will not go to them. They can choose how much insurance they want to buy, replacing part or all of the asset contributed to the CRT. This works well, especially when both parents are healthy. When they are not, they must rely on a creative alternative to life insurance for wealth replacement.

8

The Wealth Replacement
Charitable Trust

Most parents want their children to receive that which they have worked hard to create. Many will not consider a charitable remainder trust unless an economic way can be found to take care of the inheritance for the children. On occasion, the parents may be too old or too ill (or a combination), for life insurance to be a reasonable wealth replacement tool. What then?

Charitable Alchemy at Work

There is no reason why we have to look at only one type of CRT at a time; nor do we need to think only in terms of the income needs of the donors. The case of Bob and Barbara Benson provides a case in point:

Bob is a retired seventy-three-year-old engineer. Barbara is seventy-one and is very active in volunteer activities in the community. They have two married children, Tom and Susan, ages forty-eight and forty-four respectively. Bob attended college during WWII, largely on a scholarship, and he feels he should do what he can for his alma mater. He and Barbara have a good income, and their net worth is about $3 million. For years Bob has owned and managed a twenty-five unit apartment building that has a current value of $1 million, with an adjusted cost basis of $80,000. It produces about $60,000 of net income. It has been a good investment, but he is concerned that the neighborhood may deteriorate, and he is getting old enough that he would really like to sell the property. He has been to a number of seminars about CRTs, and has talked with a couple of planners and his college planned giving department. He understands how a standard trust works, and how life insurance can be used. However, he and Barbara both have medical impairments that make insurance too expensive to be economically viable. Bob understands stock market risk (volatility), and is willing to accept a variable income. He also has other sources of income, so he is not dependent on the money from the apartments.

Bob was prepared to contribute the property to a standard CRUT with a 6 percent payout, with an income beginning at $60,000 per year. The sticking point was wealth replacement. We have seen how the standard trust can work to help avoid capital gains tax and provide income. In the case of the Hendersons we saw how the NIMCRUT could help diversify and defer income, with the benefit of tax deferred compounding. What if we combined the two?

The Bensons decided to set up three trusts: one for themselves and one for each of their children as wealth replacement. Instead of contributing the $1 million property to a 6 percent standard trust, they gift a 70 percent interest in the property to a 9 percent trust. Their starting income will still be $63,000 (9 percent of $700,000), but will rise more slowly than if they were only taking a 6 percent income. Of course their net spendable income would be even lower if they were receiving the payments and buying wealth replacement life insurance.

The other 30 percent of the property, roughly the amount that they would pay to the IRS in capital gains taxes were they to sell outright, they contribute to NIMCRUTs for the benefit of each child. Bob can be the trustee of the trusts for his children and can keep the "spigot" shut off until he determines it is time to distribute income. If the trusts are initially invested for growth, and we assume the same 12 percent we assumed for the Hendersons, the value of the NIMCRUTs at Bob and Barbara's joint life expectancy of fifteen years would be over $1.5 million. The accumulated withdrawal rights would be over $700,000. Essentially, this more than replaces the $1 million apartment building. The building would have had to grow to $3 million to be worth as much to Tom and Susan, as the estate tax on the asset would have consumed 50 percent of the value had Bob and Barbara kept it.

At the time Bob and Barbara transfer the partial interest in the property to the NIMCRUTs for Tom and Susan they are making a taxable gift. The gift is the value of the income interest. Since the children are young (ages forty-eight and forty-four), the income interest is equal to about 90 percent of the value of the asset. However, the fractional interest can be discounted by approximately 15 percent. This makes the current gift about $230,000, not bad for the pool of available income that will be there in fifteen years (assuming projected investment results).

Too often people fail to look "outside the lines" for solutions to problems. The solution to the parents wanting the asset "replaced" for their children has always been life insurance. When, for any reason, it was unavailable, it often meant the gift would not be made. This is not because the families did not have donative intent, but rather that they did not feel they had enough to take care of their family if they could not replace the asset. The Wealth Replacement NIMCRUT solves that problem.

9

A Fixed Income Charitable Alternative

The Charitable Remainder Annuity Trust (CRAT)

Not everyone has the stomach for a variable income. Predictability can be more important than attempting to have income grow to keep pace with inflation. Sometimes a higher payout is needed and the donors are uncomfortable with the higher risk needed to secure higher returns, but they still want to do *something* in the way of a charitable gift and they also want to reduce current income taxes. Enter the **CRAT.**

The CRAT is easy to understand now that you have read examples of the CRUT at work. The donors still retain the income, with the remainder going to a qualified nonprofit. The trust is tax exempt, and must follow the same rules of operation as the CRUT. However, it is very different in two important areas: contributions and payout.

A CRAT is funded all at one time. After the initial funding it cannot receive any additional contributions. If the assets contributed are illiquid and do not sell quickly, the trust must distribute part of its assets to the income recipients. The donors cannot add more cash that can in turn be paid out until the original assets are sold.

The other big difference is in payout. The CRAT makes a *fixed* payment as provided in the trust document, regardless of the performance of the underlying trust assets. If a donor contributes $1 million to a 7 percent CRAT, the payments will be $70,000 per year, every year. If the trust is well invested, the corpus will grow, but the payment to the income recipients will not. If it is poorly invested, it is possible for the trust to actually run out of money before the death of the income recipients. For this reason, there is a special test called the 5 percent probability test (see Rev Rul 77-374) that a CRAT needs to pass to be a qualified charitable trust. Its effect is to negate high payout rates except for very elderly income recipients.

The tradeoff between a CRUT and a CRAT is variable versus fixed income. The CRUT income goes up and down each year with the value of the trust corpus. Over time that is likely to benefit the income recipients as well as the charities. The CRAT's level payout will not keep up with inflation and, as such, is used only by those who are more elderly or who have adequate outside income. The tax deduction is *slightly* higher using the CRUT because of the variable income versus the fixed. However, the deduction is not sufficiently greater to justify the fixed income, except for those who require a fixed income.

The CRAT is ideal for older couples who have a desire to have a specific income for whatever purpose. Many older couples, having lived through the Great Depression, have very conservative investment portfolios, with heavy cash components. Here is a good example of a multi-purpose CRAT:

George Gentle is a seventy-nine-year-old retired executive who has been married to his lovely bride Sally (age eighty) for fifty-five years. They have four children and seven grandchildren. George had a long-term career with Creative Containers and he has a nice pension of $7,000 per month with a COLA provision. George and Sally were always savers, so they were able to accumulate an estate of over $4 million. They still live in their modest $400,000 home that they bought forty years ago. They own a couple of single family residences that they rent out, and a small vacation place in the country. Most of their estate is in bonds and utility stocks. They have about $500,000 in various bank accounts, at only 4 percent interest, that has just "accumulated" over time. They would like to do something for the local college and their church, but with a big family and a lot of death taxes to pay, they just do not feel they can give. They also know they have enough income, but they are hesitant to give assets away now because "you never know what may happen." Their AGI runs $200,000 per year.

If the Gentles just continue with their present plans, the $500,000 in bank accounts will pay them taxable income, and $250,000 will be left for their family. They still cannot do much for charity today because they want to be sure the income is there "just in case." A well-designed CRAT can solve their problems.

George and Sally decide to use $400,000 of the $500,000 to set up an 8 percent CRAT that will pay them $32,000 per year. This payment will be made to them regardless of the performance of the underlying investments — it is the fixed income they want. On a gross basis it is double the $16,000 they are getting from the bank accounts, and $12,000 more than they would get if they moved the bank accounts to Treasury bills. But the story does not end there.

The contribution to the CRAT results in an immediate charitable income tax deduction of $176,182! Because they contributed cash, the Gentles can take $100,000 against this year's income because the limit is 50 percent of AGI for gifts of cash. The other $76,182 will carry over to next year. Also, as a result of contributing property with no built-in gain, they can invest most of the corpus in municipal bonds and have the exempt income pass through. The balance of the trust can be invested in growth stocks and can be held for long-term capital gain treatment. The $32,000 income distributions will be subject to an average $1,100 per year in taxes. In contrast, the $16,000 bank interest resulted in $6,400 a year in taxes!

George and Sally do not really need *more* income. They are not spending all of what they have. The CRAT now gives them the opportunity to do that which they wanted to do, but did not think they could. They know the trust corpus will go to the college after the death of the survivor, and they feel good about that. Since they do not need the excess cash flow created by the tax deductions and the distributions from the trust, they use the excess to purchase life insurance for the benefit of their seven grandchildren. The available money is enough for them to purchase $700,000 of survivorship life insurance. As the chart below shows, everyone wins.

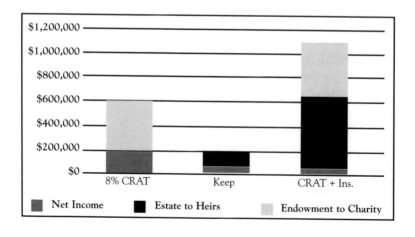

The income benefits coming from the plan show the significance of the difference. A look at the numbers is very instructive. Keep in mind that the insurance premiums are set to "absorb" the excess cash flow created, so the Gentles can retain their current income, regardless of year-to-year investment performance, and the family is never disinherited.

Comparison of Net Spendable Income George and Sally Gentle			
Year	8% CRAT	Keep	CRAT + Ins.
1	$ 72,501	$ 9,144	$ 9,501
2	$ 64,303	$ 9,144	$ 9,303
3	$ 31,176	$ 9,144	$ 9,176
4	$ 31,006	$ 9,144	$10,006
5	$ 30,822	$ 9,144	$ 9,822
6	$ 30,625	$ 9,144	$ 9,625
7	$ 30,415	$ 9,144	$ 9,415
8	$ 30,193	$ 9,144	$ 9,193
9	$ 29,958	$ 9,144	$ 8,958
Totals	$351,001	$82,296	$85,001

The life insurance policy illustrated is a universal life, giving the flexibility to make smaller or larger premium deposits based on George and Sally's perceived needs each year. Advisors need to realize the power of the CRAT and other charitable gift techniques and how they can fit into the prospective donor's wealth transfer plan. It was only by addressing the financial concerns of the Gentle family that a significant gift was created.

10

Bailing Out Corporate Earnings

Another use of the charitable remainder trust is to reduce the accumulated earnings of a C Corp on a tax-free basis. Under normal circumstances the only way for a shareholder-employee to get the earnings out of a corporation is either through compensation or dividends. When compensation in a closely held corporation starts to appear "excessive," the risk of the IRS disallowing the corporate deduction increases.[1] Pulling the earnings out as a non-deductible dividend is rarely an acceptable alternative. However, in the setting of a closely held business, it is problematical to leave excess profits in the corporation. Under IRC §531 to 535, a federal tax of 39.6 percent is imposed on earnings retained by a business in excess of its reasonable business needs where it can be shown that the corporation was "availed of for the purpose of avoiding the income tax with respect to its shareholders . . . , by permitting earnings and profits to accumulate instead of being divided or distributed." This tax is the equivalent of the highest personal income tax rate. Obviously, when a company has significant accumulated earnings the shareholder needs to get the excess out at the lowest cost possible. Where the primary shareholder also has a child or children in the business, there can be some significant benefits with a *Charitable Bailout*.

Let's look at the situation of the Good family and their corporation, Good Gosh, Inc.:

Joe Good is a sixty-three-year-old entrepreneur, who started the family furniture business with his sixty-one-year-old wife, Sue, thirty years ago. They borrowed $1,000 and put it into the business, and after a few years it became very successful. In 1971 they incorporated the business, but their basis in their corporate stock was only $10,000. They now have two sons in the business with them. They gifted each of their sons 5 percent of the stock about ten years ago. They have five stores throughout their home state of Indiana generating an average annual profit before taxes of $750,000 at the corporate level. Joe and his sons all take nice salaries, but Joe wants to slow down and take more time off. He has been told by a business broker that Good Gosh is worth about $10 million, and he and Sue have another $5 million in assets outside of the business. He is concerned about the cost of keeping the business in the family, and also about how he can get some of his value out of the corporation to use for a comfortable lifestyle in retirement. The last couple of years have seen record profits and the company now has $5 million of accumulated earnings, with over $2.5 million in cash, securities, and other liquid investments. Good Gosh's CPAs have told Joe that he needs to pay dividends or start to use the accumulations for business purposes. The family does not want to expand the business for the foreseeable future, and Joe wants to use the most tax-efficient method for getting the money out of the corporation. His AGI is $400,000 per year.

There is no way Joe can take enough of a bonus to make a dent in the accumulated earnings problem, and he wants to avoid paying dividends. If he sells some of his stock back to the corporation (a technique called a stock redemption), he can get the excess earnings out, but still may have a dividend-treatment problem.[2] However, a CRUT is a tax-exempt entity, so the dividend issue becomes irrelevant if Joe is willing to have the corpus go to charity after he and Sue die.

They decide to consider a CRUT to which they will contribute 2,000 of their shares in Good Gosh. The corporation could then buy back the shares from the trust using some of the extra cash and liquid investments. The redemption would reduce the excess accumulations, solving that problem for now. The untaxed proceeds can be diversified and invested, creating income for Joe and Sue to help offset his reduction in earning when he semi-retires. The hidden benefit is the increase in percentage ownership that his sons get as a byproduct of his reduction in ownership.*

If we assume that Good Gosh, Inc. has 10,000 shares issued and outstanding, we know that Joe owns 9,000, while his sons have the other 1,000. Based on a $10 million valuation, his 90 percent is really worth $9 million. When he contributes 2,000 shares to his CRUT, those shares represent a *minority interest,* and will be subject to a discount for tax purposes.[3] If we assume a very modest 20 percent discount, the fair market value of the transferred shares would be $1.6 million. Once the 2,000 shares are redeemed by the corporation there will only be 8,000 shares outstanding. Joe's 7,000 shares represent seven-eighths of the outstanding shares, or 87.5 percent. The sons' share of the future increase in value of the corporation has gone up 25 percent (from 10 percent to 12.5 percent). Joe and Mary now have $1.6 million in a CRUT that is no longer subject to the

---

*The sons will own a higher percentage of the corporation, but it should be noted that the value of the corporation will be reduced as cash is distributed to the CRUT.

business risk, can provide them with an income, and will be out of their estate.

This type of corporate buyout works even better than the sale of normal capital assets because the gain if it were done in a taxable fashion would be treated as ordinary income, with a top federal tax bracket of 39.6 percent versus 20 percent. The tables that follow illustrate the benefits of an 8 percent standard CRUT versus a taxable partial redemption, with the assumption that Joe earns 10 percent on the net proceeds.

Comparison of Benefits Summary
Mr. and Mrs. Good

A. Input Assumptions:

	Unitrust	Sell and Reinvest
Type of Technique	Unitrust	Sell and Reinvest
Time Period Projected	1997-2020	1997-2020
Income Payout Rate	8.00%	All Income
Income is Paid	Quarterly	Quarterly
Investment Period Measured by	2 Lives	2 Lives

B. Contributions:

	Unitrust	Sell and Reinvest
Fair Market Value of Property	$1,600,000	$1,600,000
Income Tax Deduction Permitted	**$288,944**	$0
Tax on Sale	$0	**$720,000**

C. Cash Flow:

	Unitrust	Sell and Reinvest
Income During Life (after taxes)	$2,462,377	$1,323,779

D. Estate for Heirs:

	Unitrust	Sell and Reinvest
Gross Value of Estate	$0	$880,000
(+) Life Insurance Death Benefit	$0	$0
(−) Estate Taxes	$0	$484,000
(=) Net Estate for Heirs	$0	$396,000

E. Benefit Summary:

	Unitrust	Sell and Reinvest
Net Income + Net Estate equals Total Family Benefit	$2,462,377	$1,719,779
(+) Endowment to Charity	$2,239,145	$0
(=) Total Benefit	$4,701,522	$1,719,779

Comparison of Net Spendable Incomes
Mr. and Mrs. Good

Year	8% CRUT	Sell and Reinvest	Benefit of CRUT
1	$54,283	$156	$54,127
2	$157,199	$57,549	$99,650
3	$91,885	$57,549	$34,336
4	$88,476	$57,549	$30,927
5	$89,783	$57,549	$32,234
6	$91,108	$57,549	$33,559
7	$92,452	$57,549	$34,903
8	$93,816	$57,549	$36,267
9	$95,199	$57,549	$37,650
10	$96,602	$57,549	$39,053
11	$98,025	$57,549	$40,476
12	$99,468	$57,549	$41,919
13	$100,933	$57,549	$43,384
14	$102,418	$57,549	$44,869
15	$103,925	$57,549	$46,376
16	$105,453	$57,549	$47,904
17	$107,004	$57,549	$49,455
18	$108,576	$57,549	$51,027
19	$110,172	$57,549	$52,623
20	$111,790	$57,549	$54,241
21	$113,431	$57,549	$55,882
22	$115,096	$57,549	$57,547
23	$116,785	$57,549	$59,236
24	$118,498	$57,549	$60,949
Totals	$2,462,377	$1,323,779	**$1,138,594**

The large difference between years one and two is the result of the income tax deduction created by the CRUT.

Self-Dealing Considerations

Any time there are dealings between a charitable trust and anyone even remotely related to the trust (the donors, etc.) great care must be taken to research the possibility of a self-dealing violation.[4] The law is very broad in the area of self-dealing, and running afoul of the rules would create a major disaster. The Internal Revenue Code considers Good Gosh, Inc., a "disqualified person" as it relates to Joe and Sue's CRUT.[5] Fortunately, there is an exception to the self-dealing rules for a redemption of stock by the corporation, so long as the same offer is made to all stockholders owning the same class of stock, and the redemption is for fair market value.[6] So, to avoid the self-dealing problems, Good Gosh will have to offer to redeem the stock held by the sons at the same price and terms offered to Joe. But, given the goal to pass more of the company on to the sons, they would not be interested in having the corporation buy back any of their stock. Even so, this type of translation needs to be very carefully structured to avoid self-dealing rules and to be sure it is not treated as a step transaction. This type of related party deal has more inherent tax risk.

11

Solving Special Problems

Benefiting Domestic Partners

A growing number of people are choosing to live together and not marry. Some are homosexual and cannot legally marry, while others are heterosexual and for whatever reasons decide not to marry. They often have no children and want to leave money to charity after the death of both partners. Frequently, one of the two partners has the larger asset base, and is concerned about the other partner's income at the time of the first partner's death.

Domestic partners have a special problem when it comes to estate and charitable planning. Simply put, they are ineligible for the marital deduction, so taxes are due at the first death. The tax cannot be deferred to the survivor's death. A CRT can be of tremendous help. The partner with the appreciated assets can contribute property to a charitable remainder unitrust that will provide income for his or her life and that of his or her partner.

This is the point at which the attorney drafting the charitable trust must be very careful. Since the couple is not married, the trust must provide that the donor reserves the right to revoke the income interest of his or her partner. This right of revocation makes the gift of the successor income interest an incomplete gift. If it were not subject to a right of revocation, it would be considered a completed gift at the time the trust is funded. That would then require the filing of a gift tax return and the payment of gift tax, or the use of part of the applicable credit. This would be undesirable and unnecessary.

They must exercise additional care in the amount contributed to the trust and the growth of the trust assets. At the death of the donor (who is also the initial income recipient), the value of the trust corpus will be in his or her estate. The present value of the charitable remainder interest will be eligible for the charitable estate tax deduction, leaving the income interest as a part of the taxable estate. If that amount, along with other assets being left to the partner or other friends and relatives, exceeds the amount that can be sheltered by the credit, estate tax will be due at the death of the first partner. The nice thing about the CRT is that the partner can receive an income from the assets, with a reduction in the taxable value for the charitable remainder.

Capturing Income Tax Benefits

Quite often, a couple or an individual will make a decision to leave a significant amount to charity as part of their will. Most nonprofit organizations actively solicit such gifts (called bequests). The bequest is non-threatening as it is usually revocable, and it takes nothing from the donors during their lifetimes. The gifted property will not be subject to estate tax at death because of the charitable estate tax deduction. The problem is that many donors do not realize that they are missing valuable income tax deductions.

Consider the following example:

George and Mary Generous have built a nice estate over the years. George is a seventy-five-year-old retired contractor. Mary, also seventy-five, is a retired school teacher. They have two children who are both comfortable, with good work and stable families. Their net worth is $6 million, a third of which is invested in municipal bonds to avoid having to pay extra taxes. They also own a couple of small apartment buildings. They are not spending all of the income (their AGI is $150,000) that their assets generate. Their current will provides that one-third of their estate will go to a public charity to fund scholarships in their name.

When the second spouse dies, at least $2 million will go to charity. The estate of the second spouse to die will receive a charitable estate tax deduction for the total gift. However, they really feel "overburdened" by taxes. Their CPA suggested they make a major gift to charity right now, but as people who grew up in the Depression, they are not comfortable giving too much away, even though they realize they may not need the money themselves.

This is another example of how a charitable remainder trust can be very useful. George and Mary have a significant amount in municipal bonds, primarily because they do not want to pay additional tax on their income, especially because they are not even spending what they make. They design a CRUT to make sure they retain the income, just in case, while still giving the principal to charity when they die.

A 7 percent CRUT gives them a tax deduction equal to 40.7 percent of their contribution. They decide to contribute $500,000 to this trust, generating a current charitable income tax deduction of just over $200,000. Since their muni bond portfolio has plenty of bonds with little or no gain, they can contribute cash without recognizing any capital gain. By doing so, they can deduct approximately $75,000 the first year, as they are limited to 50 percent of AGI. The balance of the $200,000 total deduction is carried forward, and they can use it over the next year or two.

Because they contributed just cash and bonds with no appreciation, there is no income in tier one (ordinary income), or tier two (capital gain). That provides them with increased investment flexibility, as they can retain some of their municipal bonds as a part of the trust's balanced investment portfolio and receive the income tax free. If the trust divides the portfolio between low-yield stocks and municipal bonds, George and Mary can receive an income that is partially tax exempt, and partially taxed at the lower capital gains rates.

What have they accomplished? Well, by using the CRUT they will receive current income tax deductions for money that is destined to go to charity anyway. The $200,000 deduction will save them about $80,000 in income taxes. If that alone were not ample reason, they can also invest for a higher total return, selling winners whenever appropriate, and never pay income tax on profits they do not actually receive.

The Term of Years Trust

A charitable remainder trust can be for life or for a term of years not to exceed twenty. Entities can establish CRTs, but they must be for a term of years. With the new 10 percent rule discussed earlier, the term of years trust is likely to be used more often. Most individuals want a life income, and younger people who are eligible for a 5 percent payout trust might balk at the low payout needed to qualify the trust. A twenty-year term trust could have a payout rate of

11 percent, more than double the joint life trust.

Let's take a couple and look at an interesting opportunity:

> David and Diana Dinks are a hard-charging young couple. David is forty and Diana is thirty-five, and they are both successful executives. They have been married for ten years, have no children, and have decided they like the freedom, so they have decided that they will not start a family. They enjoy their limited time off together traveling, and they both enjoy the challenge of their jobs. They spend freely out of their combined income of $300,000. Their net worth is now $3 million, including $1 million of zero-basis stock in David's former employer, Killer Programs, Inc., a NASDAQ-listed company. They were getting ready to put $500,000 in a 7 percent CRT early in 1997 when their planner told them to wait until later in the year. The new 10 percent test made it impossible to use a 7 percent joint life trust.

If the Dinks sell their Killer stock, they will pay almost $145,000 in federal and state capital gains taxes. They would prefer a CRT, but are unwilling to use the low, 5 percent payout rather than the 7 percent they were considering. So, they decided to do a twenty-year term trust with an 11.5 percent payout. At a 7.6 percent current 7520 rate, the trust will pass the 10 percent remainder test.

The trust starts out paying almost 50 percent more than the 7 percent trust would. Right now David and Diana do not need all the income, so for the first five years they take the net after-tax distributions from the trust and allocate them to a variable life insurance policy on their lives. From the sixth year through the fourteenth year they spend what the 7 percent trust would have provided, and put the rest into the variable universal life (VUL) contract (see chapter 13 for a discussion on types of life insurance). The inside buildup of the VUL is tax-free, and assuming the same 12 percent return as we have on the CRT, the value when the CRT terminates in twenty years will be approximately $650,000. If the same returns are assumed for life, the Dinks can withdraw $1,545,000 over the following twenty-five years.

While the withdrawals from the VUL are slightly less than those from the 7 percent CRUT, they are close to what would have been available. At this point they **cannot** create a 7 percent trust because it fails the 10 percent test, so the only alternative to the CRT is a sale. If the Dinks sell their stock and pay the tax, they only have $355,000 left. Again, at the same 12 percent return, if they take the same net income available from the twenty year trust, **they go broke in the sixteenth year!** While the term trust is not quite as beneficial to the Dinks as the life income trust would have been under the old rules, it is still far better for them than an outright sale.

SECTION THREE
Increasing the Family Legacy

12

Making Real Gold Look Like Fool's Gold

The Family Limited Partnership

Section 2031 of the Internal Revenue Code provides that a tax is paid on the transfer, at death, of all the assets owned by a decedent at the time of death. The tax is levied based on the *fair market value* of the assets. It is well settled that fair market value is "the amount at which the property would change hands between a willing buyer and a willing seller, neither being under any compulsion to buy or to sell, and both having reasonable knowledge of relevant facts."[1] Everyone knows the value of cash. Publicly traded securities (stocks and bonds) also have a readily ascertainable market value. The difficulty of valuing other enterprises provides interesting opportunities for sophisticated wealth transfer planning.

The enterprise that is considered most suitable for establishing a fair market value significantly less than the intrinsic value of the underlying assets is called a *Family*

Limited Partnership (FLP). The FLP has become increasingly popular over the past few years since the Internal Revenue Service agreed that the valuation of a family enterprise will be treated similarly to those in which a family is not involved.[2]

Let's look at an example of a situation where an FLP works wonders:

> Harry Jackson is a sixty-year-old real estate developer. He and his fifty-five-year-old wife, Sally, have three children, ages thirty-two, thirty, and twenty-six. They have over $9 million of investment real estate net of a $1 million mortgage, $1 million in stocks, and other assets with a total value of $2 million. The real estate produces a net income of $600,000, and the stocks yield another $50,000, significantly more than Harry and Sally need to support their lifestyle. They have a living trust and want to pass as much as possible to their children at the lowest possible transfer tax cost. One of their sons is a real estate broker, while the other is a dentist. Their daughter is a homemaker and her husband is a pediatrician. Although Harry and Sally care about their children's spouses, they want to be sure the assets remain in the Jackson family. Harry also wants to be sure he and Sally retain management control of the assets.

The key elements here are the desire to retain control of assets, while also wanting to transfer wealth at a reduced cost. This creates a great opportunity for the use of a family limited partnership. The Jacksons form a new entity called Jackson Enterprises, L.P. Harry and Sally will initially own it as both limited partners and general partners. The general partners will own 2 percent of the capital of the new partnership, and the limited partners will hold the remaining 98 percent. The management of the partnership will be fully controlled by the general partners.

The FLP is designed to be very restrictive. The limited partners cannot cause the partnership to distribute income.

In order to liquidate the partnership and distribute its asssets, all limited and general partners must concur. The limited partnership interests cannot be sold or otherwise transferred without consent of all other partners, essentially meaning that all a transferee can receive is that provided an assignee and not the full rights of a limited partner. If you think about it, who would want to own anything so restrictive? That is just the point and the goal. A well-designed FLP will have units that are about as desirable to an outsider as a home adjoining Love Canal. Since the family is not trying to raise money from outsiders, they are concerned about dissipating "value," rather than creating it. They want the valuation to be as low as possible because the only thing the valuation currently affects is the amount of a gift or bequest.[3]

The amount that is considered to be subject to transfer taxes is the fair market value of the property transferred. In the case of the Jackson real estate, we know the value is $9 million, net of the liability. But what happens when the properties are owned by the new partnership? What happens when the "property" given to the children is a minority interest in the family limited partnership and not a direct interest on the real property itself? Remember, the limited partners cannot simply liquidate the interest they own and get at the underlying assets. The landmark case in this area is the *Harrison* case which was decided by the Tax Court in 1987. It is important to understand and has been included in Appendix B for those interested in reading the facts and the opinion.

Limited partnership units in the new Jackson enterprise will be appraised by a business appraiser based on their value, not necessarily that of the underlying assets. When considering the value of limited partnership units there will be discounts given for lack of marketability, lack of control, and a minority interest discount. Until the early 1990s, the IRS fought valuation discounts, even though it usually lost in court. In the *Newhouse* case in 1990, the Tax Court said,

"Ignoring discounts for lack of marketability is *contrary* to long-established valuation methods well accepted by the Courts in cases presenting the value of stock in closely held corporations." The Service's attitude was that families would always vote together, so the restrictions were essentially meaningless. We all know that families often are less than unified, and even the IRS finally gave up the fight in 1993 in Rev. Rul. 93-12 discussed earlier.

Given the current judicial and administrative positions, specialists in this area are comfortable planning for a 30 to 60 percent discount in a well-structured FLP that contains the restrictive provisions most business appraisers feel justify such discounts. In *Estate of Gordon B. McLendon v. Commissioner* (77 AFTR2d 96-398) the Fifth Circuit Court of Appeals, in reversing the Tax Court, pointed out that the interests actually transferred were *assignee* interests, not *partnership* interests. The court opined:

> Both the gift and estate tax issues turn on categorization of partnership interests Gordon transferred. The Estate suggests that the interests transferred could only be remainders in 'assignee' interests in the partnerships, not the actual partnership interests themselves. Texas law, relied on by the Estate, prohibits the transfer of partnership interests without the agreement of the other partners.

The Tax Court agreed with the IRS that the interests transferred were partnership interests and that it was all part of a plan to avoid estate taxes. The Estate responded with non-tax management continuity and other reasons, as well as its reliance on state law. In a biting reprimand the Appeals Court said:

> Viewing the transaction at face value, it is evident that the Tax Court's neglect of Texas law was unfortunate. *The Tax Court does not sit to create its own rules of business organization governance* (emphasis added).

Where the Internal Revenue Code has not superseded state law, the tax consequences of a transaction must depend on the nature of the deal under state law. Accordingly, we look to Texas law as well as the various agreements to evaluate the transactions executed among Gordon, Bart and the Trust.

As this illustrates, there are technical issues having to do with state laws that may make it desirable to set up an FLP in a state other than the domicile of the family. The decisions on all of these important issues mandate the use of an attorney who specializes in this area of the law.

In the Jackson's case they designed an FLP that would provide the greatest discount possible. They contributed the real estate to a new FLP in which Harry and Sally were the initial limited partners, and Harry was the general partner. The FLP requires that 100 percent of the limited partners, as well as the general partner, agree before the partnership can be liquidated, with the assets distributed to the partners. No partner can transfer units to another party without the consent of all other partners.[4] In the event that a limited partner's interest is acquired by anyone, through litigation, etc., they can only be an assignee, and cannot be admitted as a substitute limited partner.

With everything in place, Harry and Sally contributed the real estate to the FLP in exchange for the general and limited partnership units. The partnership issues 1,000 limited partnership units. After consulting with counsel, Harry and Sally decide to make gifts totaling $1.2 million, using up their unified credits. Ordinarily the $1.2 million would represent 12.24 percent of the limited partnership units ($1.2 million divided by the total value of $10 million times 98 percent — the other 2 percent is general partnership interests). However, due to the various discounts available, Acme Appraisal Associates had opined that the gifted units are only worth 50 percent of their prorata value of the entire entity.[5] Consequently, Harry and Sally can give the children 24.8 percent of the LP units and not trigger gift taxes. They get $2.4 million of *real* value out of their estate, but only use the $1.2 million sheltered by the applicable credit.

Harry will still control all aspects of the business. He decides to take a minimal salary of $50,000 because he really wants to reduce his income, as it just builds the estate even more. Now, of the $600,000 net income from the partnership, approximately $150,000 will go equally to the three children, all of whom are in a lower tax bracket than Harry and Sally. The 15 percent income tax differential alone will save the family unit $22,500. In addition, Harry and Sally had been gifting $60,000 per year to the children for the payment of survivorship life insurance premiums. Now the children can pay the premiums out of the after tax partnership distributions. In addition, instead of Harry and Sally gifting cash for insurance premiums, they can give $120,000 worth (remember the 50 percent discount) of FLP units and continue to reduce the value of their estate. The children will benefit from the growth of the partnership units they own. Not bad.

The FLP also has the non-tax benefit of protecting the transferred assets from potential creditors. Since the agreement prohibits the transfer of limited partnership units, all that creditors can get is what is called a "charging order." It gives them the right to attach any income that flows out to the limited partner against whom they have a judgment. However, since Harry controls the partnership, he might suspend distributions leaving nothing for the creditors. There could even be taxable income without any cash to pay the taxes. This makes an FLP interest almost toxic waste in the hands of an unwanted creditor, so they generally avoid looking for such collateral. Many practitioners recommend family limited partnerships primarily for these non-tax benefits.

Alas, even with this magnificent, near-magic technique, it has its warts. Assets that have a low adjusted basis and are heavily mortgaged (resulting in mortgage in excess of basis), cannot be transferred to an FLP without triggering taxable gain at the time of transfer. Also, there are potential traps in some states with property tax reassessment (a major concern in California), transfer fees, etc. These problems can often be overcome, and with a 55 percent estate tax as the alternative, some current transfer costs may be well worthwhile. The family limited partnership is complex. However, if **significant** tax dollars are to be avoided, if disinheriting the IRS is the goal, putting up with some complexity in the design is part of the price that must be paid. It is really no different from the complexity of design needed in modern buildings to help them stand up to earthquakes, storms, etc.

13

The Life Insurance Decision

After using a panoply of planning opportunities, the reality is that life insurance will be a part of most plans. The reason is very simple: it makes sense. For wealth transfer planning, life insurance provides the leveraged, guaranteed benefits that provide the mortar that holds the bricks in place. Life insurance is not about savings, nor is it an investment. Proper plans employ life insurance to provide the needed cash at the *specific* point in time at which it is needed. Probability and statistics are great when there are large numbers of people playing, but no sound estate plan can risk being wrong. Life insurance in the context of the wall around your wealth is used for many different things. In an example in chapter 6, when Tony and Linda set up a CRT they increased their income by transferring the lot to the CRT. However, after they die, charity receives the remainder interest, effectively taking the asset from their children. A survivorship life insurance policy will guarantee the children receive a cash benefit at the same time as the corpus of the CRT goes to charity. The benefit could mature tomorrow, or in thirty to forty years. It does not matter, as death creates both the need and the solution. This book contains several examples of life insurance used for such "wealth replacement."

Life insurance is best used in combination with some of the value-shifting techniques that are the reinforcing mechanisms in our wall. The various forms of split interest trusts and valuation-adjustments take time to work. Unfortunately, longevity, as opposed to life expectancy, is unknown. So, life insurance provides a hedge. Proper planning assures people that they will always retain wealth during their lifetimes to assure adequate income and to provide financial security and opportunity. The retained wealth that they choose to pay to heirs creates tax, and the insurance pays the tax so the assets do not need to be liquidated.

Sometimes people do not want to "complicate" their lives with the sophisticated planning discussed in this book. Their main goal is to keep everything simple. But wealth carries with it the burden of the payment of a great deal of money in a short period of time, creating a financial mess. Over twenty years ago Ben Feldman, one of the greatest life insurance agents of all time, said, "When you walk out for the last time, you'll leave a mess that needs to be cleaned up. Pay me less than the cost of your janitor, and I'll walk in with the cash to clean up the mess." Simple? You bet.

Once the decision has been made to purchase life insurance as a part of the estate plan, there are still a number of other important decisions that will have to be made. It will be very important to properly coordinate the life insurance with the rest of the estate plan. For example, if the wife is the grantor of a GRAT* and she dies before the end of the GRAT term, taxes may be due at that time, and a policy that pays only at the death of the surviving spouse will be of little use.

---

*See discussion on the use of a GRAT starting on page 112

Types of Life Insurance

Most consumers are aware that there are two basic forms of life insurance: term and permanent. As the names imply, "term" is for a limited number of years. When you buy term insurance it is like renting your home. You have no equity. The rent will go up over time, and when you are old you could find the rent too high and end up homeless. The reason the premiums **must** go up over time is that the term premium just covers the risk of dying (the mortality cost) during the stated policy term. As people age, the risk of dying increases each year. The older the insured, the higher this risk premium must be. It is for this reason term insurance is rarely used in estate planning, as it becomes too expensive to continue as one reaches age seventy and above. There is little benefit in paying for insurance that is unlikely to be in force at life expectancy or beyond.

Permanent insurance is an umbrella term that refers to a type of policy that will usually have level premiums that are higher than term premiums in the early years, but significantly lower in the later years. Permanent coverage comes in many forms. There is whole life and universal life, participating and "interest-sensitive," single life and survivorship, and finally fixed life and variable life. A client, then, may be offered a variable survivorship whole life policy, or an individual universal life policy. The simplest way to unwind this confusing web of names is to define each.

A *whole life* policy is one that is designed to provide a **guaranteed** death benefit and guaranteed cash value. The policy is usually structured so the cash value equals the death benefit at age 100. They say that the policy "endows" when the cash value equals the death benefit. If a policy endows, the benefit is paid even though the insured is alive, usually creating an income tax problem. One of the reasons this policy can have a level premium is that as the cash value grows over time, the *risk* to the insurance company decreases (and therefore less premium is charged for the risk element). This is because the basic policy has a level death benefit, part of which is offset by the cash values.

The whole life policy, if issued by a "stock" company (one with shareholders) will generally be an *interest sensitive* policy. The contract will guarantee to pay interest of at least 4 percent on the cash value, but can credit higher rates. Over the past fifteen plus years that these policies have existed, interest rates credited have ranged from a high of 13 percent to a low of 5.5 percent. The credited interest generally tracks 1 to 2 percent below interest rates on bonds and mortgages. In addition to the interest-crediting rate changing periodically, the mortality charges (also called the risk premium) are subject to revision. They can vary between the rates guaranteed in the contract itself and a lower charge if company experience so warrants. If interest rates are higher than the guaranteed rates, the premiums on the policy may be able to be suspended — they were often said to have "vanished." However, in the low interest rate environment of the 1990s, they all "reappeared" and policyholders needed to begin paying premiums again.

An insurance company owned by its policyholders is called a mutual company. Its whole life policy is referred to as *participating* whole life because the policyholder participates in the profits of the company. The participation takes the form of a *dividend*, which under law is a return of premium. The dividends can be used to reduce premium, buy additional paid up life insurance, buy term insurance, etc. A participating whole life policy tends to be more flexible in its design than an interest-sensitive whole life. However, it also tends to be a bit higher in guaranteed premium because the gross premium includes a charge for the "ownership" of the company.

The next important category deals with the life or lives insured. Before 1981, the affluent always had a tax liability at each death. Then, the law changed and allowed taxes to be deferred until the death of the surviving spouse, assuming the plan took advantage of the "marital deduction." Instead of needing insurance to pay taxes at each death, the insurance only needed to pay at the second death, and *survivorship* life insurance became the primary estate planning insurance product. It is a contract on the lives of two people, usually husband and wife. It pays a death benefit only after the death of both insureds. In most cases premiums are paid even after the first insured dies, although some companies have riders that waive the premiums at the death of the first insured. The policy can be in the form of an interest-sensitive whole life, participating whole life, or universal life.

Survivorship life is a less costly alternative designed for the estate planning market. Since both insureds have to die before the policy pays its benefits, the probability is that it will be a longer time that the insurer will have the use of the money. This is reflected in lower premiums, even when one of the insured has health problems making him or her "uninsurable." The policies are now issued to much older ages, with individual insureds as old as eighty-five not being uncommon. In the chart below you can see the difference in rates for individual policies and survivorship policies for those in the prime estate planning years.

Before the late 1970s the insurance industry operated

	100% Whole Life	50% WL, 50% Trm	25% WL, 75% Trm
M60/F55	$16,780	$15,238	$14,256
M60	$33,090	$19,450	$21,469
M70/F65	$30,220	$28,087	$26,433
M75/F70	$42,000	$37,492	$35,175

Rates are for a $1 million policy issued on a preferred, non-smoker basis. The examples shown are from a major carrier and are indicative of what is available in the marketplace. It is assumed the premiums are paid until death for the blends. One hundred percent whole life premiums would be able to be suspended at a point in time, depending on the performance of the policy, or the premiums could be continued and the benefits increased.

with a very simple portfolio of whole life products. While participating whole life had existed for over 100 years, there was no interest-sensitive product. Stock companies issued a guaranteed cost contract that paid only 3 to 4 percent interest on the reserve (cash value). With soaring interest rates and the general availability of money market funds, companies were forced to find a way to pass on some of the increased earnings or risk having the policyholders withdraw all the cash to invest at higher returns. The answer was the *universal life* policy.

In a universal life, or UL, policy, the policyholder pays a premium from which the insurance company subtracts an expense charge. The company then subtracts the monthly "risk premium" to cover the cost of term insurance for one month. The balance is then credited with interest that can be adjusted monthly. With a UL product the policyholder shares the upside of higher earnings and improving mortality (lower costs associated with fewer people dying than expected), as well as the downside of lower interest rates, etc. The UL policy is not built around guarantees, and is designed so the insurance remains in force so long as there is adequate money in the policy for the monthly risk and expense charges. While flexibility is a good thing, the normal UL policy does not **guarantee** a death benefit forever as does a whole life policy. This author has found that most people dealing with insurance for their estate plan want to be certain of the amount of insurance.

During the 1990s interest rates have dropped, while the stock market has reached new highs. This has spurred the development and sale of the newest generation of life insurance products, *variable life*. With a variable life policy the cash value grows (or shrinks) as a function of the returns of subaccounts (essentially mutual funds) selected by the policyholder. Variable life can be either variable whole life or variable universal life. In 1995, most fixed policies, ones where the reserves are invested in the general account of the insurer, interest credited dropped to about 6 percent.

The stock subaccounts of most variable life policies increased over 25 percent. This can create some real benefits for policyholders, but stocks and bonds can go **down** as well as up. If the policyowner makes poor investment decisions, the policy *could* lapse without value. To mitigate this risk, many companies offer "no-lapse" guarantees at certain premium levels.

The decision as to what type of product to use is very important and quite complicated. The whole idea behind life insurance is the transfer of risk. When the plan includes conventional (non-variable) life insurance, the risks include the fixed-rate investment returns of the insurance company and the solvency of the insurer. Variable life provides greater control of the investment decisions and significantly reduces insurer solvency issues, while the policy owner takes on the investment risks. Over the long term, diversified equity portfolios have always provided a higher rate of return than fixed income investments.

No one **likes** to pay insurance premiums, and people want to believe they can find the real bargains. However, with life insurance it is vital to make sure your insurance lasts longer than you. Some insurance salespeople will illustrate low premiums that are unlikely to be able to support the policy, without always explaining that much higher premiums will be required unless all current assumptions are met. People can be fooled into believing that they can get the same thing for substantially less. While there are differences amongst policies and companies, the lowest bid is often missing something. Caution is important when deciding what to buy and how much to pay.*

The way the premiums are lowered, regardless of

---

*In 1997 most states adopted guidelines issued by the National Association of Insurance Commissioners. These NAIC Guidelines require significant disclosure about the assumptions underlying various insurance illustrations. While this does help by assuring a common illustration format, it is still very complicated and consumers should work with experienced professionals who they feel are working to find the most appropriate product and premium structure.

whether a whole life or UL contract is used, is by decreasing the guaranteed part of the policy, taking up the slack with additional term. The problem is that term (this is the pure risk element) protection costs more each year as the insured gets older, with no offset for increasing cash value or interest credits. If a $1 million policy is designed to have $500,000 of cash value at age eighty, it is also supposed to have only $500,000 of "risk" or term. Let's assume the cost of $1,000 of risk at age eighty is forty dollars. The risk premium in the above example would be $20,000 (500 times forty dollars). If 6 percent were being credited on the cash value, there would be a credit of $30,000. That is enough to pay the risk premium and still have the cash value grow. But what if years earlier the policy had been sold with a low premium so that the cash value at age eighty is only $200,000? There are 800 units ($1,000 per unit) of risk at a cost of $32,000, and the $200,000 of cash value at 6 percent only generates $12,000. Now there is a $20,000 decrease in the cash in the policy, and the problem will quickly accelerate, causing the policy to self-destruct unless some hefty additional premiums are paid.

Life insurance is simply one of the materials used in the construction of the wall around family wealth, and the wall can only be as strong as the materials used in building it. No one would ever buy homeowner's insurance that only covered fires that occur on Monday, Wednesday, or Friday. If it existed, it would be a cheaper policy, but we intuitively understand that we want protection no matter what day a fire breaks out. In modern life insurance marketing, policies have been designed to let the buyer assume more of the risks of changing economic conditions and mortality, just like our fictional homeowner's policy would let the purchaser take the risk that a fire will not start on a Tuesday. In estate planning it is very important to make sure that the policy will be available and affordable under all reasonable assumptions, not just current ones.

Ownership of Life Insurance

Life insurance is considered an asset, just like stocks, bonds, or real estate. The big difference is the significant increase in value at death. Under section 2042 of the Internal Revenue Code, life insurance is included in the estate of an insured who had at the time of death any "incidents of ownership." The incidents of ownership include the ability to change beneficiaries, borrow the cash value, surrender the policy, etc. Since the goal of most life insurance in estate planning is to provide tax-free benefits to pay taxes at death, planners usually do everything possible to keep the policy out of the estate of the insureds.

The most common method of keeping life insurance out of the estate is to have the contract owned by an irrevocable life insurance trust for the benefit of the children and/or grandchildren. The trustee must be someone other than the insured, and the insured cannot have any interest in the trust assets. By keeping the economic interest of the policy removed from the insured, the proceeds will usually avoid inclusion in the estate. Due care must be taken to avoid a number of traps that can cause inclusion of the benefits in the estate of one insured or the other.

The irrevocable life insurance trust (ILIT) should be in place and the initial owner of the policy. If the policy is transferred into the trust after issue and death occurs within three years after the transfer, the proceeds will be included in the estate of the deceased insured. However, even though the trust should be in place before the policy is applied for, the total plan needs to be well thought out, as the trust is *irrevocable* and cannot be changed after it is signed and funded.

The ILIT usually receives the money used to pay the premiums as a gift from the insureds. In order to qualify the gifts for the $10,000 annual exclusion, the trust is drafted with "Crummey" provisions. The name comes from the case

Clifford D. Crummey v. Comm (397 F2d 82, 9th Circuit 1968). Each beneficiary has a right to withdraw the money contributed for his or her benefit for a limited amount of time each year. This withdrawal right is referred to as a Crummey power, and if properly established qualifies the gift for the annual gift tax exclusion of up to $10,000 per donee.[1] The trust stays in effect until after the death of the surviving spouse, using the tax-free proceeds of the insurance to buy assets from the estate. The estate uses the cash to pay the estate taxes due nine months from the date of death.

The difficulty with this trust is that it is irrevocable and cannot easily adapt to changing conditions in the family. Sometimes the parents will let the children own the policies outright, but then there are potential entanglements with divorce, lawsuits, etc.

An alternative that is now becoming more popular is the family limited partnership. Yes, the FLP that contains much of the family investments can own the insurance. Often a separate partnership is established primarily for the purpose of acquiring the necessary life insurance. Younger generations own most of the partnership units, with the parents often being the general partners. While a small amount of the policy will be included in the estate based on the parents' interest in the FLP, that is a small price to pay for the flexibility retained in a totally revocable partnership.

14

Keeping the Fruit and Giving the Tree

From an estate planning standpoint, the problem is the shear size of the transfer tax. At 55 percent it is designed to be confiscatory as a way to prevent over-concentration of wealth. Most people cannot afford to give up income as well as assets, yet they do not want the assets to go through the estate-tax wringer. While there are risks associated with all planning strategies, the use of different split-interest trusts can be very helpful in allowing the older generation to maintain an income for most of their lives (the fruit), while giving away the assets (the trees).

Planning for the retention of income can be tricky. Section 2036(a) of the Internal Revenue Code throws back into a decedent's estate any assets that were transferred while the decedent retained a life interest. So, just as with the QPRT that will be discussed in the next chapter, any arrangement that provides income must be carefully designed and implemented.

When the Parents Still Need Income

The GRAT

There is a way to transfer assets to heirs after a specified period, while retaining an income in the interim. This technique is detailed in §2702 of the Internal Revenue Code.[1] It is called a **G**rantor **R**etained **A**nnuity **T**rust, or GRAT for short. With a GRAT the parent or parents transfer assets they own to a trust with a fixed term of years. It must be for a period less than the expected life of the parents for reasons previously mentioned. The person transferring the assets is called the *grantor*. The income stream *retained* by the grantor is a fixed percentage of the value of the assets transferred,[2] and it is considered the *annuity* interest. The children, or remainder beneficiaries, will receive whatever assets remain in the trust at the end of its fixed term.

The trust is irrevocable, so the children should receive "something" at the end of the trust term. That vested remainder interest constitutes a **gift** at the time the parents establish and fund the trust. So, how is the amount of the gift determined? Well, you start with the *value* (as we have previously noted, this term is very important in building a wall around family wealth) of the assets transferred to the trust. You then calculate the actuarial value of the income interest retained. For example, what is the value today of an income stream of $100,000 per year for twelve years? The biggest determinate is the interest rate assumed. What percent of the assets is represented by the $100,000 annual income? That payout rate is important because the GRAT is assumed to earn the "7520 rate," which is 120 percent of the monthly average of the five to seven year treasury notes. Since the calculation assumes a modest current interest rate, if the GRAT paid out 12 percent while earning 6 percent, the assets would be depleted over time. However, if the trust earns (and total return is the key, not just yield) more than the required payment, it will grow in value even though the calculation assumes the corpus will decrease. The remainder interest calculation is further affected by the possibility that the grantor will die during the trust term and the trust will revert to his or her estate.[3] The bottom line is the fact that the children do not get the assets until later, and the parents are drawing money out whether the trust earns it or not, leading to a significant present value discount. Many GRATs are designed so the value for gift tax purposes is less than 10 percent of the assumed value of the trust at inception. Let's take a look at an example:

Don and Mary Goodliver are a healthy, active couple who are seventy and sixty-eight respectively. They have been married for forty-five years and have three grown children and five grandchildren. Their parents all lived beyond age eighty-five. They have an estate valued at $6 million, with about half of the estate in Don's sporting goods company, Goodliving, Inc. It is an S Corp that Don started thirty years ago, and it is now being run by his two sons, Joe and Harry. His stock is held as separate property. Joe and Harry each have 10 percent of the stock in Goodliving, Inc. that they received through gifts over the years. When Don retired last year he had to give up his $240,000 salary, but 80 percent of that still comes to him by virtue of his ownership of 80 percent of the S Corp stock. He has about $1 million in his rollover IRA, but wants to take minimum distributions for now and let it grow. He really wants Joe and Harry to have the business after he is gone. He would not mind them getting it earlier if he felt that he and Mary would have enough income to travel, ski, and generally enjoy life. Without Don's salary, the business has a net income of about 10 percent of its current value of $4 million, plus it is growing in value another 10 percent per year.

Designing a GRAT

The first consideration in designing a GRAT for Don and Mary will be the term of the trust. If they try to retain the income too long, the chances increase that one of them will die during the trust term. That would cause the whole plan to blow apart because the income will have been retained for life instead of a term of years less than life. Remember that the estate tax is a tax on the transfer of a decedent's assets at the time of death. Included in what a decedent owns are any assets transferred in which he or she retained a *life* interest (IRC §2036). Even though the GRAT has a measured term that is **meant** to be less than the life of the grantor, if death occurs before the end of the trust term, the value of the trust at the date of death will be back in the estate. Not good. So Don and Mary want to select a term that, accidents aside, *should* end several years before death. They feel comfortable "betting" on a twelve year term. By that time they may slow down and travel less. Also, the IRA will likely be larger and they can draw more out after that time.

Before establishing GRATs to give them an income, Don will "give" Mary half of his stock. It will become her separate property. No gift tax will be due on the transaction because gifts to spouses are fully sheltered by the marital deduction. After the gift they will each own 40 percent of the corporation. The true value of their 80 percent interest is $3.2 million.

What about the annuity rate? Don wants them to receive at least the $240,000 per year he was getting in salary. On the estimated $3.2 million of their interest in the business, that is only a little over 7.5 percent. The fair market value of a minority interest in a closely-held corporation will be subject to discounting, similar to limited partnership interests discussed earlier. While the discounts are not likely to be as much as they would be with FLP interests, they should be one-third or more.

If Don and Mary's combined stockholdings were to be

valued at $2.2 million ($3.2 million less a little more than a 30 percent discount), the $240,000 they need would be 10.91 percent of the "adjusted" value. A twelve year 10.91 percent GRAT for Don on his 40 percent interest creates a current gift of $314,750. A similar trust for Mary creates a current gift of $292,000. That is a 79 percent discount from the stock's "real" value of $3.2 million, but uses up half of their unified credits. Don wants it to be a smaller gift for gift tax purposes.

Increasing the Annuity

Since Don and Mary do not want to increase the risk of the plan not working by lengthening the term of the trust (because of the risk of dying during the trust term), all they can do is increase the amount of the retained income. If they take 14 percent instead of the 10.91 percent (for a total of $308,000 per year — .14 x $2,200,000), the taxable gift is reduced to $155,000, a more appealing number. But where does the money come from to pay the annuity to them if the cash flow is not available from the corporation? The law allows the payments from a GRAT to be in cash or "kind." That means the trust could pay them some cash and some stock. One problem with that is that each year the stock must be valued to determine how many shares go back to Don and Mary. Also, when the trust terminates Don and Mary will own stock that they wanted to get rid of. Even so, they will be significantly better off. Because the payment is fixed at $308,000, and the company is growing (as will its earnings), there will be very little stock that will go back to Don and Mary over the twelve years.

A positive feature of the GRAT is that it is a grantor trust for income tax purposes. That means that Don and Mary will pay the income tax liability on the profits from the Goodliving shares in the trust (just as they do now). Even though the children will eventually receive the stock left in the trust, Don and Mary will pay all the taxes so that the trust grows without the tax burden. If they receive shares in any given year because the cash flow is inadequate to pay the annuity payment, the transfer is not considered a taxable sale or exchange.

Spreading the Risk and Increasing the Benefit

There is a greater chance that either Don or Mary will die during the next twelve years, than that they both will die. They took advantage of the opportunity to mitigate that risk and still accomplish what they wanted to do by having Don give half of his stock to Mary and each setting up their own GRAT. If one dies, the other's GRAT is still out of the estate.

What Have They Accomplished?

If Don and Mary outlive the twelve-year terms of the GRATs they set up, they will have truly built a wall around much of their wealth. Don could have retained the stock and received the distributions from Goodliving, Inc. Let's assume that Don and Mary die in an accident together fifteen years from now. The corporation, as projected, would have grown in value at 10 percent per year, making its value $16,709,000. Even if they receive a 20 percent marketability discount on their 80 percent holding (no minority interest discount), the value would be $13.4 million and the tax would be $7.35 million.

By establishing the GRATs and currently making gifts of minority stock, they gave only $155,000 of the $1.2 million they can give before paying transfer taxes. If we then assume that that is $155,000 more on which they would pay estate tax, the cost would be $57,750 in the 55 percent bracket. That cost is **99.2 percent less** than retaining the stock until death. If they both died before their respective trusts terminated, they would be no worse off than if they did nothing.

Don and Mary would be without income from the stock (or the GRAT) after the twelve years. But, if the rollover IRA grew at 6 percent more than the minimum withdrawal requirements, it would have doubled to $2 million over the twelve years. Don and Mary would then be eighty-two and eighty, and at a 10 percent total return the IRA would give them $256,000 per year for another thirteen years before running dry. They still have other assets, and it appears the benefits of the GRAT significantly outweigh the costs or risks. Even if the company does not grow in value at all, the tax savings are dramatic.

There is one disadvantage to the GRAT that some practitioners will focus on. Just as with other split-interest gifts (and outright gifts), the stock will not receive an increase in basis for capital gains purposes. However, when the children can avoid a 55 percent estate tax, and at most pay the 27 percent (including state) capital gains tax, it makes economic sense.

Lifetime Income With a GRAT-NIMCRUT Combo

Too often people look at planning opportunities on a single-problem, single-solution basis. Unfortunately, that paradigm usually leads to inaction because there are problems created by the implementation of one technique that dissipate the enthusiasm for it. Using Don and Mary's GRAT example, their income from the GRAT would cease after twelve years. What if they needed income, and did not have a sizable IRA?

Earlier we covered the deferral benefits of the NIMCRUT. If instead of an IRA Don owned appreciated assets that he was willing to sell, he could establish a NIMCRUT. It could be invested in such a way as to grow for the twelve year term of the GRAT, without generating much distributable income in the interim. When the income from the GRAT stops, the NIMCRUT could begin to distribute income that would substantially replace that lost at GRAT termination. Don and Mary would have a lifetime income, while both the GRAT assets and the NIMCRUT assets would have been removed from their estates. The confidence that adequate income will be available for life, not just the GRAT term, makes it much more likely that the major gift to the children will actually occur. At the same time a significant charitable gift can be created.

SECTION FOUR
Letting Charity
Take the Lead

15

The Qualified Personal Residence Trust (QPRT)

Affluent families often have a personal residence or vacation home that they want to get out of their estate. It often has a significant market value. The 1990 tax act included a new provision that provided for what has become known as a qualified personal residence trust (QPRT).[1] It is very similar to a GRAT in that the grantors retain an "income interest" with the remainder going to a younger generation. The difference is that the asset contributed must be a personal residence, and instead of receiving income the grantor simply continues to live in the house for the term of the trust.[2]

The important distinction in a QPRT is that the asset must be a *qualified residence*. Treasury Regulation Section 25.2702-5 deals with the definition of a qualified residence and restricts it to a primary residence or vacation home (as defined by IRC §280A). The QPRT technique can be used for a maximum of two such properties. It cannot be used for rental property, nor can it be used for large tracts of land that are not an important part of the qualified residence. For example, if a couple owned a 5,000 acre ranch with a home on a corner of it, they could not transfer all 5,000 acres to a QPRT. There are letter rulings dealing with farms and ranches and other examples that can help one understand the IRS's position.

The QPRT is designed as a grantor trust, making its income tax neutral. The transfer of the house to the trust does not trigger any gain or loss. If the house is sold during the trust term, the gain will be taxed to the grantor. If the grantor has the $250,000 exclusion available for the sale of a personal residence, it will apply to the sale of the house in the trust. The real reason for the QPRT is estate tax reduction.

The best way to understand a QPRT, as with many of the other trusts we have discussed, is to look at a couple of examples. First, let's visit with John and Helen Marshall:

> John is an eighty-five-year-old retired professor and his wife, Helen, is an eighty-one-year-old former sculptor. Their estate, all of which is community property, is almost $4 million, with their spacious home constituting 20 percent of the total ($800,000). They have more than adequate income, but do not want to give away income-producing assets, as they want to be absolutely sure they have "enough" for the rest of their lives. John's health is fair, and Mary is in excellent health. They are currently making annual cash gifts to their two children, and they want to reduce the tax impact on their estate.

With a QPRT, as with a GRAT, if the grantor dies during the term of the trust, the asset is included in the estate.[3] Because the QPRT is a split-interest trust with a risk that it will be thrown back into the estate of the grantor, the longer the term of the trust and the older the grantor, the greater the calculated retained interest. The greater the retained interest, the smaller the current gift. Because

Currently

Current Value $800,000

1. Mary transfers to seven year QPRT

Qualified Personal Residence Trust

Value Retained $559,000

2. Current taxable gift to children is $241,000

3. Mary lives in house for next seven years, just as if nothing had been transferred

After Seven Years

1. Ownership of house goes to children

Estimated value $1,053,000 at 4 percent growth rate

2. Mary pays children fair market rent as long as she lives in the house

the remaindermen do not receive the asset until a point in the future, the gift is not eligible for the $10,000 annual exclusion. Finding the "right" formula for the trust term and the grantor can be a real challenge. In the Marshall's case, there is a strong probability that Helen will outlive John. Playing the odds, they decide to transfer the house to Helen, who will then transfer the house to the trust. There is no tax due on the transfer from John to Helen, as a transfer between spouses is protected by the marital deduction. The transfer of the house to the QPRT does not trigger any taxable gain, so its basis in the trust is the same as the basis of the grantor. The QPRT will run for seven years, during which time John and Helen will continue to live in the house just as they do now. On the surface the trust is transparent. John and Helen maintain the residence, pay the utility bills, and generally ignore the existence of the trust that holds title to the property. At the end of the seven years the trust will terminate and the house will go to their children.

The law provides for a formula approach to determine the amount of the gift to the children. It uses the same applicable federal rate that is used in calculating interests in the other split interest trusts (GRATs, CRUTs, etc.). Part of the calculation considers the possibility of death during the trust term. In Helen's case, at age eighty-one and with a 6.8

Percentage of Value Deemed Taxable Gift to Children

	5 Year	10 Year	15 Year	20 Year
Age 60	63.26%	38.46%	21.99%	11.48%
Age 70	57.17%	29.85%	13.28%	4.62%
Age 75	52.22%	23.28%	8.08%	1.98%
Ages 60/60	68.26%	45.57%	29.06%	17.04%
Ages 75/75	64.74%	35.02%	14.14%	3.78%

Assumes 7.8 percent 7520 rate. The QPRT provides the greatest gift tax reduction when the 7520 rate is higher rather than lower. Also, as can be seen in this chart, the benefits are greater for single life versus joint life QPRTs.

percent 7520 rate, the discount for the interest retained is 67.8 percent. The deemed value of the remainder interest in the seven year trust is $241,472. The table above shows the various taxable remainder interests (value of 1.0 minus the retained interest) at different ages and trust terms.

Assuming Helen lives for seven years, the house will belong to the children at a gift tax value of $241,472. If the value of the house were to increase 4 percent per year over the seven years, it would then be worth $1,053,000. The table below shows the estate tax savings at seven years assuming different rates of growth of the house. This analysis focuses on the estate tax savings and does not consider possible capital gains tax exposure. While capital gains tax can be significant, the rate on capital gains is less than 40 percent that of the estate tax, and it can be deferred or eliminated.[4]

	4% Growth	6% Growth	8% Growth
Value in 7 years	$1,053,000	$1,202,900	$1,371,100
Estate Tax Savings	$446,200	$528,800	$621,300

After the seven years, if John and Helen* would like to remain in the house, they must pay fair market rent to the children. Pay rent? Why would anyone want to pay rent to their children to remain in their "own" house? Actually, for wealth transfer purposes this is a mini-bonanza. The rent is not considered a gift, as John and Helen are paying market rent to the real owners of the property. If they did not pay market rent, yet lived in the house until they died, the value of the house would be back in their taxable estate because it would be considered a transfer with a retained life interest.

John and Helen will pay rent that will be taxable to the children. However, they can also set up a trust for the ben-

---

*As the house was first transferred to Helen, it is technically her responsibility. If John dies before her, as expected, she will have to pay full rent as long as she remains in the house.

efit of the children. The trust, referred to as a "defective" or "intentional" grantor trust, is treated like the grantor's property for income tax purposes, while not for estate taxes.[5] Since a person cannot pay him or herself taxable income, the rent paid by the grantors creates no tax liability to anyone. This is a very creative way to get the benefits of estate tax exclusion while avoiding unnecessary income taxes. There are a number of interesting articles on defective grantor trusts and they have been discussed in great depth at major estate planning institutes.

With John's health not being the greatest, there remains the possibility that he will need to move to a nursing home or residential care facility before the seven years are up, and Mary might go with him. If the trust sold the home at that time, the trust becomes a grantor retained *annuity* trust (GRAT), and Mary would be entitled to an income for the duration of the trust, with the remaindermen receiving the investment assets of the trust. The income is calculated based on a percentage of the net value of the house when it was contributed to the QPRT. The percentage income is based on the 7520 rate. For example, if the net assets in the trust are $1 million and the 7520 rate is 8 percent, Mary would receive $80,000 per year for the remainder of the seven year term.

The QPRT rules allow for two trusts, with each having a "qualified personal residence." This is very helpful, especially for families who have expensive vacation property that they want to keep in the family. Since the entire family already enjoys the use of such property (with the parents owning it and being the primary residents), this type of property is ideally suited for contribution to a QPRT. Let's look at another example:

> Ed is a seventy-year-old retired business-owner. His wife, Marion, is sixty-one. Their combined net estates are valued at $6 million. Of this, about $1.2 million is in a lovely vacation home in Hawaii. It is free of

any debt, and is used by Ed and Marion about six months per year. Their children occasionally join them, and everyone loves the house, with its view of the beach and proximity to a great golf course. Ed and Marion plan to use it extensively for the rest of their joint lives, but Marion feels she will spend less time there once Ed dies. Given the age difference and the fact that Marion's mother died at age ninety-six, everyone figures that she will outlive Ed, and should make it to age ninety.

As with John and Mary, it seems most prudent to first transfer the house to Marion and let her establish the QPRT. The marriage is strong and Ed is not worried that Marion will throw him out or get a divorce (but this is important to discuss). Ed and Marion want as little financial dealing with their children as possible, so they want the trust term to be long. They started by looking at a twenty year term. That decreases the time that Marion would have to pay rent, but increases the probability of inclusion in her estate. So, they decide on a "rolling" QPRT. The entire house is put in the trust, but it comes out a piece at a time. One third will be distributed free of trust in eighteen years, with another third in twenty years and the balance in twenty-two years.

By doing this they hedge the risk of her not living more than twenty years, while taking some risk because she must live twenty-two years to get the whole property out of her estate. The twenty year QPRT at Marion's age results in a gift of only 10.5 percent of the property value, while the rollout QPRT is 10.7 percent, virtually identical from a gift tax standpoint. The real issue is how to hedge the risk of dying too soon. Even creating a rollout QPRT does not solve the problem because there are no guarantees. Here is a case where life insurance is well-suited to solve the problem, as discussed in chapter 13, dealing with the life insurance dilemma.

16

More Charitable Wealth Transfer Alternatives

The Wealth Transfer Charitable Lead Trust

We spent considerable time going over a number of examples of how a charitable **remainder** trust can be used to accomplish a number of things more efficiently (with more benefit to the donors), while ultimately controlling social capital by keeping it in the community rather than paying it out in taxes. The reverse transaction, the Charitable Lead Trust (CLT), is a fabulous wealth transfer tool that is used less often, probably because it is less understood and does not follow the tenet of charity beginning "at home." Also, since it is not a tax exempt trust and cannot avoid capital gains taxes on the sale of appreciated assets, it is not thought of from a transactional standpoint.

The CLT, like the CRT, is a split interest trust. In both cases a charity must be a beneficiary. While the general purpose of the CRT is to retain income and give the remainder to charity, the CLT seeks to give charity the income (called the "lead" interest), with either the donor or the heirs receiving the remainder. The CLT can be used primarily for charitable purposes, where the nonprofit receives income for a certain term, after which the donor gets the assets back. This is often used when a donor wants to fund a current project or make a pledge of a specific amount per year over a fixed period. Since the donor ends up with the assets at the end of the trust term, there are no wealth transfer benefits when it is designed in this manner. However, the estate planning use of the CLT comes when the heirs of the donor are the remaindermen.

The most frequently used CLT is the charitable lead *annuity* trust (CLAT). There are two types of CLATs, referred to as grantor or non-grantor lead trusts, the most common being the non-grantor lead. In the non-grantor lead, the donor gets no current income tax deduction. The trust pays taxes at trust rates on its net income, after receiving a deduction for the income paid to charity. Ideally, the trust is managed so as not to produce much in the way of taxable income in excess of the payout. The grantor lead creates a charitable income tax deduction for the present value of the income stream going to charity, but unlike the non-grantor trust, this trust's income is fully taxable to the grantor, with no additional deduction for the payments made to charity.

Just as with the CRAT, this type of annuity trust pays a fixed income determined at the outset of the trust, as opposed to an income that varies with the value of the underlying assets. At the end of the trust term the assets, be they more or less than at the formation of the trust, will usually pass to the children. Since the payout to charity is fixed, the more the trust grows in value, the more the heirs will receive. Because it is not a tax exempt trust, planning with a CLAT is more complicated than with a CRT, but as you will see, the rewards are worth the effort. Let's see what George and Mary Leader do with a CLAT.

George is a sixty-eight-year-old retired executive and Mary is proud to be a sixty-five-year "young" mother of four and grandmother of seven. The Leaders have a cohesive family and George and Mary want to maximize the estate for their children. They have a net worth of $6 million, with about $4 million in actively managed stocks and bonds, $1 million in rental real estate, and $1 million in other assets. Their income is over $200,000 per year, and they are contributing $40,000 each year to various charities. Several years ago they gave their children $1.2 million because they were concerned the unified credit would be cut to shelter only $400,000. They do not need additional income, and, as a matter of fact, they end up saving money each year. Mary has had some health problems. She really wants to work with her children, sharing her philosophy of being responsive to the needs of the community. She and George would also like to have their children receive some significant assets in ten to fifteen years, even if they are still alive.

The idea of a CLAT appeals to them. The income given to charity from the CLAT could be in lieu of the annual gifts they are currently making. If they give $500,000 of their assets to the trust and give 8 percent to charity each year, they will continue their existing gift pattern uninterrupted and the children will get the assets. If the trust runs twelve years, just about the time they would like the children to receive some money, the calculation at a 7 percent 7520 rate (remember this rate, which changes every month, is used to calculate the interests in all split interest trusts) results in a current taxable gift of $364,584. Since there is other gifting they want to do as a part of their overall planning, that is more of a taxable gift than they would like to make at this time, at least for the CLAT portion.

After hearing about the benefits of a family limited partnership, George and Mary decide to establish an FLP and contribute a portion of it to a CLAT. The FLP starts out with $4 million of real estate and securities. Their appraiser informs them that the value of a minority interest in limited partnership units will be subject to a 50 percent discount for lack of marketability, etc. So, if they transfer 25 percent of the FLP units, the "real" $1 million value will be deemed worth $500,000 for transfer tax purposes. The total return anticipated on the partnership assets is 10 percent per year. To give the same $40,000 to charity requires only 4 percent of the real value. After considering the estate planning benefits of the CLAT, George and Mary decide to increase the gift to charity to $62,500 per year. That is 6.25 percent of the true value of $1 million, and 12.5 percent of the deemed valued of $500,000. With the higher payout rate to charity (12.5 percent versus 8 percent), the trust can terminate in twelve years and the taxable gift is only $7,162. This saves gift taxes (at 50 percent) of over $173,000 and the asset base being transferred to the children is almost double!

The 7520 rate affects CLATs in the opposite manner than it affects CRTs in that the lead, or income interest, goes to charity. Here, the higher the 7520 rate, the higher the charitable payout needs to be to secure the same reduction in the amount of the gift to the children. This table shows the highest annuity rate that will still pass the 5 percent probability test..

The key here is that the trust is paying to charity a fixed income that is projected to be less than the total

Percentage Lead Payment Needed to Pass 5% Test

	7520 Rate		
	6.40%	**7.60%**	**8.40%**
10 Years	13.50%	13.90%	14.55%
15 Years	10.15%	10.85%	11.51%
20 Years	8.55%	9.40%	10.12%
25 Years	7.72%	8.60%	9.36%

return on its assets. The assumed return on the asset base is 10 percent, or $100,000 in the first year. Since only $62,500 was withdrawn to make the charitable payment, there is $37,500 "excess" left in the trust, which will grow as well. The larger the trust grows, the smaller the $62,500 becomes as a percentage of the trust, and the faster the trust will compound. In our example here, the children will receive $1,801,911 of assets, at a transfer tax cost of $3,581 ($7,162 present value of remainder interest at a 50 percent tax rate).

This trust is a taxable trust that pays tax on its earnings. However, it gets a deduction for the amount paid out to charity. So long as the portfolio is not turned over frequently, the trust is not going to show income much in excess of the amounts paid to charity. And since George and Mary can be the general partners of the FLP, they can bleed off some of the excess earnings as salary so the partnership and the trust show less reportable income.

Charitable lead trusts, like all of the other instruments we have covered, are simple (well, maybe not really simple) materials used in the construction of a solid wealth transfer plan. The trust that did more to bring attention to the CLAT than any other that I am aware of, was the trust created upon the death of Jacqueline Kennedy Onassis. The "JOLT," as it was called (for Jackie O Lead Trust), was established under her will. It was a *testamentary* lead trust as opposed to the more typical *inter vivos*, or living trust. Jackie's estate would receive a charitable estate tax deduction of over 90 percent, since most of her estate would have gone to a CLAT that for twenty-four years would pay an annuity interest to her foundation. At the termination of the trust, the assets would have gone to her grandchildren. However, the lead trust was to receive that portion of her estate that was "disclaimed" by John and Caroline. For a number of reasons the children decided to pay the tax and take the money instead of disclaiming in favor of the CLAT. It was not funded, and one of the most famous charitable trusts in history never began operation.

The Lead Trust
and Grandchildren

The CLAT is a great tool for passing wealth and controlling social capital. It works best in those cases where the value of the asset increases without triggering taxable current income. It also has been most fitting in those situations where the trust corpus will go to children rather than grandchildren. The reason for this is that when the trust goes to grandchildren rather than children, the value for generation skipping transfer tax purposes is calculated at trust termination, not the formation of the trust, and can create a major GSTT problem.

In the example of George and Mary Leader, the value of the gift to their children was $7,162 and was considered a taxable gift at the time the trust was created. The projected value on termination of $1,801,000 is out of the estate and is not subject to further transfer tax. However, if this were to be left to grandchildren, it would be subject to the 55 percent generation skipping transfer tax (assuming the allowable exemption had already been used). That would mean $990,000 in tax at the end of the twelve-year trust.[1] One way to mitigate the GSTT problem is to use a Charitable Lead *UniTrust* (CLUT) instead of a CLAT.

The difference between the two trusts is that the CLUT pays a variable amount to charity, rather than the fixed payment from a CLAT (the same as we discussed with the CRUT versus the CRAT). The problem is that the better the performance of the trust assets the more that will go to charity, and that is not the only reason why people establish wealth transfer lead trusts. It solves the GSTT problem, but at the cost of automatically having a smaller corpus.

17

Keeping the Family in Charity

Philanthropy can be totally passive or very active. Many families experience great emotional benefits from becoming more active in the distribution of their wealth. Not only does involvement in their causes make the gifts more meaningful, but involving the family in the process can significantly improve the family dynamic. Focusing on what to do for the good of others is more rewarding than deciding who gets what within the family. According to one philanthropist I have heard, "Intelligently giving away money is far more difficult than making money."

There are many approaches to philanthropy. Professor Paul Schervish of Boston College has researched various types of donors. Russ Prince has also done a great deal of research on affluent individuals and their involvement in the community. The reality is that the transfer of wealth is the transfer of values, and the more the senior generation can share their feelings with the younger generations, the more likely their values will be continued after their death.

Financial "Parenting"

Paul Comstock, 1996 President of the National Conference on Planned Giving, wrote an insightful article titled "Financial Parenting Through a Family Foundation."[1] In it he presented the concept of "financial parenting" through the involvement of all family members, ages twelve and up, in the processes of running a private foundation. Unlike some people who have suggested that a relatively small private foundation could employ all of your children, Paul focuses on the personal development benefits of having the family work together for the good of the community. Many practitioners who have approached families about the idea of involving younger generations in philanthropy have had very positive responses.

However, you need not set up a family foundation to enjoy the benefits that come from the financial parenting concept. One suggestion I have made to a number of clients who regularly make charitable gifts, is that they involve the family in the annual giving process. For example, let's say each year you give $5,000 to various causes and organizations. You have two children and three grandchildren, ages twelve to sixteen. At Thanksgiving (or some other time when the family can get together) you offer to make $2,500 available for gifts to the nonprofits chosen by each of the five younger family members — $500 each. You will write the checks and the contributions will be made in the name of the family member selecting the charity. Sound easy?

There is a catch, and here is where the learning comes in. Before you will agree to fund a selected project, the person advocating that gift must "report" to all of you on why he or she feels the gift should be made. What will the charity use it for? How efficient is the nonprofit in the use of its money? Is it a qualified public charity? Has the person advocating the gift read the most recent Form 990 (tax return)? Is he or she committed enough to the organization to volunteer his or her time periodically?

This is a simple, cost-free way to involve everyone in a project that they can all be proud of. The pay is not financial, but the ultimate rewards are greater than money. The pride that one grandmother experienced was tremendous when she saw how hard her twelve-year-old granddaughter had studied before ultimately deciding that her share should go to a food bank. For the twelve year old, the good feeling that came from knowing that her decision would help feed a number of needy families in her community was unlike any other experience. The only excuse for not working together is that it does take time and energy. "The children are so busy with other things," is something I hear all the time. "Kids want to be with their friends and aren't interested in this sort of stuff," is also a stock answer. But isn't that also why we **should** try to have the entire family work together? I have even heard stories where this type of project, initially pushed by the senior generation, helped battling, dysfunctional families come back together. For many families, it would be a very worthwhile experiment. Then, if it works well and the senior generation decides as a part of their wealth transfer planning to fund a private foundation, they would be comfortable knowing that the younger generations were well-trained.

Private Foundations

Private foundations provide the ultimate in legacy and control for those who feel this is important. However, the potential for abuses in private foundations makes for special, restrictive rules.[2] A private foundation does not receive any substantial support from the public at large, usually being funded by its creator, with occasional contributions from a few friends. This lack of public support and concentration of control in the foundation's creator and his or her family can lead to substantial abuses that could benefit the founder's family, so Congress passed legislation aimed at reducing potential abuses.

There are two types of private foundations: operating and non-operating. The most common is the non-operating foundation. It makes grants to public charities, rather than actually dispensing food and services like an operating foundation. Many of America's great foundations, including the Packard Foundation, the Kellogg Foundation, and the Ford Foundation, are all private, non-operating foundations.

One of the disadvantages of being a private foundation is that it must pay an excise tax equal to 2 percent of its "net investment income" for the year.[3] While this may not seem like an excessive tax, keep in mind that most foundations make their distributions exclusively from net income, so any tax hurts. For many the choice of a private foundation is predicated on *control* issues, not only as to who gets what, but as to investments, personnel, etc.

While control is important, it comes at an extraordinarily high compliance price. Because their creators often abused private foundations, in 1969 Congress added the myriad rules that private foundations still have to follow. The sections applying to self-dealing are laden with "land mines" that can blow up in the face of the unwary. When §4941 is violated, the penalties can be draconian. The problem with the self-dealing rules is that they are so broad that what may seem like an ordinary, arms-length transaction between the foundation and its creator will usually be a violation. Most philanthropists who establish private foundations have some entrepreneurial spirit and want to be "involved." Too often that involvement can lead to infractions of the rules.

When the self-dealing rules are violated, the "self-dealer" is required to pay a penalty tax of 5 percent of the value of the self-dealing transaction, even though it was not intentional and the transaction was corrected or reversed. If the act of self dealing is *not* corrected within the taxable year, the penalty is increased to **200 percent** of the value of the transaction. Can you imagine the consequences if the transaction cannot be reversed? The 200 percent penalty tax is the most severe penalty tax to be found in the Internal Revenue Code!

It would be easier to avoid innocent transgressions if the creators of the foundation only had to worry about self-dealing acts. However, §4941 forbids acts of self-dealing by *disqualified persons*.[4] Given the potential number of disqualified persons (including entities) and the myriad acts of self-dealing, this can be a major disincentive for someone who just wants to control his or her social capital.

The private foundation is also burdened with additional rules that restrict its "entrepreneurial" investment ability. Often an owner of a closely held business may want to contribute his or her interest in the business to the foundation. This is heavily restricted by IRC §4943, which imposes a tax on excess business holdings that is similar in its magnitude to the tax imposed on acts of self-dealing. Essentially, a private foundation cannot own a closely held business. Even when there is an opportunity to earn a good return through a higher risk investment (not owned or controlled by a disqualified person), such investment may create a problem. It could be considered a "jeopardy" investment that is taxed under IRC §4944.

The non-operating private foundation, even after obeying all of these special rules, is still restricted to making distributions to public charities or private operating foundations. It cannot give its own scholarships, do its own research, etc. It is strictly an entity set up to give money to other nonprofits, which in turn are active charities. Given the other alternatives available, the private foundation fits fewer family objectives.

Supporting Organizations

Private foundations sound appealing to many entrepreneurial people because they provide the ultimate in *con-*

trol of social capital and foundation investments. However, they also have the disadvantages of tighter government scrutiny, lower tax benefits, and major restrictions on the assets that can be held by the foundation. These issues became even more significant when taxpayers lost the ability to deduct the current fair market value of some appreciated assets contributed to private foundations. A great alternative is the *supporting organization.*

A supporting organization (SO) is considered a *public* charity rather than a private foundation. It is provided for by IRC §509(a)(3). "So long as the supporting organization is organized and operated exclusively to support one or more publicly supported charitable organizations, it qualifies as a public charity regardless of whether its support comes from the general public or from a single contributor."[5] While the technicalities of supporting organizations are well beyond the purview of this book, the ways in which they can be used to control social capital will be very instructive.[6] Even though they are frequently established with significant sums of money or assets, they can be efficiently established and operated with as little as $1 million.

An SO is really a hybrid. Usually established by individuals who want to retain significant influence over the operation of the organization, its board must be controlled by people outside the famly (they must constitute a majority of the board) and it also must *support* specific public charities. As you will see in our example, neither of these restrictions creates major disadvantages. The SO is becoming far more user-friendly as creative specialists develop strategies for its use.

The SO has the benefits available to public charities because its resources must be used to support qualified public charities, and the assumption is that there will be adequate public oversight. A major benefit is that the SO is not subject to the self dealing restrictions that burden private foundations. The SO can make arms-length, properly secured loans to family members. It can enter into business transactions with family members (known as "disqualified persons") without concern about the draconian penalties imposed by IRC §4941. It need not be concerned with the jeopardy investment or excess business holdings restrictions that burden private foundations. These advantages can easily outweigh the negative of the lack of absolute control by the family.

Let's consider the following example:

> Warren Caring, age seventy-three, and his wife Susan, age sixty-two, have built a successful construction firm with an estimated fair market value of $30 million. In addition, they have investments worth another $10 million and a lovely home valued at $2 million. Caring Enterprises is a "C Corp." Ninety percent of the stock is owned by Warren and Susan, with the other 10 percent owned prorata by their four children, three of whom are active in the business. Warren and Susan have an annual gross income of $500,000. They have been active in community affairs and are very concerned about education. They have also been involved with the local theatre company, a fledgling community theatre which is a 501(c)(3) organization. They want Caring Enterprises to continue to be family-run and their three children want to stay employed there. They know that the $20 million plus they will owe in estate taxes if they do nothing will be a major problem, and they would like to direct that much of that social capital be used to support the local schools and the theatre company.

One example of how an SO can be valuable to a family is when there is a valuable family business that the senior generation wants to be managed by children who are active in the business, but the estate tax would be a major burden for the estate. The parents estate plan could provide that a significant part of the stock of the family enterprise be contributed to the family's supporting organization. The bequest would qualify for the charitable estate tax deduction, significantly reducing the estate tax burden. The

Carings decided to recapitalize the corporation and create a class of non-voting preferred stock (with an 8 percent non-cumulative dividend) as well as a class of non-voting common stock.

The Carings then establish The Caring Foundation, a charitable organization to support the local school foundation and the community theatre. They fund the corporation (which qualifies as an SO) with $2 million par value of the preferred stock, which was valued at $1.2 million after the various discounts associated with minority interest, lack of liquidity, etc. The directors of the SO — there are five — are Warren, his son Jack, Tom (a longtime friend), Sally Stagefright (the director of the theatre company), and George Generous, a member of the school board. Each year Caring Enterprises will pay a dividend of $160,000 to The Caring Foundation and the directors will decide how the money is to be split between the school foundation and the theatre based on the needs of the respective organizations.

At Warren's death he leaves another $2 million of the non-voting preferred and his share of the non-voting common to The Caring Foundation. Of his voting stock he leaves enough to his children to fully utilize any remaining unified credit, with the balance going to a QTIP trust for Susan's benefit. The stock left to the SO is deducted from his estate because of the charitable estate tax deduction, and the stock left to the QTIP is eligible for the marital deduction. This entire transaction is free of transfer tax.

When Susan dies the stock in the QTIP trust can also be left to the SO, creating a transfer of the stock with no transfer tax. The only problem with this plan is that the directors would have significant control of the corporation, and the corporation would have an ongoing commitment to pay dividends to the SO. With this in mind, the children will own survivorship life insurance on Warren and Susan with the intent to use the proceeds to purchase the stock from The Caring Foundation. The purchase must be at *fair market value*, likely less than *prorata* value for all the reasons we have previously discussed.

In this situation we can also use the corporate purse to help fund the needed life insurance. Caring Enterprises will enter into a split dollar agreement with the children (or more likely a trust for their benefit), and pay the bulk of the annual premiums.

Donor Advised Funds

The Donor Advised Fund (DAF) is an extremely valuable tool for philanthropists and their families. Many families want to have the benefits of their own charitable fund, but do not want the expense and administrative headaches involved in a private foundation or supporting organization. They also may not want to be involved in research on needy organizations or in evaluating numerous grant requests. For these families the DAF may be the answer.

A Donor Advised Fund is essentially an earmarked account with the assets held as a part of the general funds of a public charity.[7] The nonprofit invests the assets along with its own, providing professional investment advice at a cost-effective price. The family is not involved in managing the money, and they do not need to be involved in tax reporting, etc.

The nonprofits that offer DAF programs are already involved in operations that assist a wide number of programs, or in evaluating grant requests that come from other charities. They are prepared to share their expertise with the family, greatly simplifying the process.

Donors are not restricted to the charity's own programs or to grant requests that come to it. In most cases the donors can request that money from their DAF be sent to any qualified organization for use anywhere in the world. The key word, however, is "advised." The donor can *advise* the charity to spend money on a particular project. The final decision rests with the board of the nonprofit where the funds reside.[8] If the donors could demand that money be spent as they wish, it would be more like a private foundation and obviously would not fit in the structure of the public charity.

A wide variety of public charities offer DAF programs. Most community foundations are set up to administer them, and they actively encourage participation by local donors. Some have geographical restrictions, but many do not. The community foundation will generally charge from 1 to 3 percent to offset the cost of administering the DAF program for the donors. The foundation's motivation in establishing donor advised funds is that it gets an opportunity to meet with the donors and encourage gifts in the community or to the foundation's unrestricted fund. A number of organizations that I have talked with often find that more than 50 percent of the distributions from the DAFs they administer are used for programs that are supported by their general funds.

One of the early participants in DAF programs was World Vision, an international Christian relief organization. It introduced the program as a way to encourage entrepreneurial philanthropy and to become closer to its donors. World Vision usually requires that at least 10 percent of the money contributed to a DAF be given for World Vision programs. Whenever donors do not decide how to spend all of the income available, the DAF sponsor becomes the obvious beneficiary.

The number of organizations offering DAF opportunities has mushroomed in recent years. A quick search of the World Wide Web uncovers programs established by Cornell University and by Heartland Trust (established by a banking institution for obvious business development purposes). Several of the local Jewish Federation offices also offer donor advised funds. For time-constrained donors who still want themselves and their families to have input, a DAF is

an ideal remainderman for a CRT, as well as a logical lega-
tee under the donors' testamentary documents.

In order to have a donor advised fund that is "advised"
by the appropriate people, the donor needs to sign an agreement with the charity. The agreement will spell out the
costs, terms, etc. Also, if the parents want to restrict the
types of organizations they want their heirs to be able to
benefit, such restrictions need to be set out in the agreement.

18

Making it Work —
The Final Phase

Wealth transfer planning is a term that practitioners use for more advanced "estate planning." But regardless of what it is called, it deals with two things people do not like to think about — death and taxes. The tax part is easy because most affluent individuals will talk all day about reducing or eliminating taxes. Most of them do not want to talk about death, especially their own. The wealth transfer process need not focus on death if it instead encompasses the transfer of personal values. This shifts the focus to sharing the senior generation's philosophy with younger generations, with discussions of what the family and community legacies should be. With the gifting that also is a part of the planning, parents are able to watch their children enjoy some of the money during their lifetimes.

All ideas presented in this book do little good if they are not properly implemented and periodically reviewed. There are a number of major roadblocks in the way of the completion of a sophisticated plan that might include a number of the legal and financial techniques we have

discussed. One of the biggest is a lack of understanding of
how the techniques work. Hopefully, the examples we have
covered provide help to reduce this problem.

Another obstacle is the inherent complexity of both
design and implementation. Many people, especially as they
get older, do not like to deal with complex ideas, much less
complex entities that they must deal with over the years.
Advisors have a responsibility to clients to help make the
complex more understandable, and to help, whenever possible, to make the implementation and administration tol-
erable.

There is no question that families can "keep it simple"
and pass ample assets to heirs through the use of life insurance. Charities can continue to benefit because donors care
enough to make gifts regardless of the tax implications. But
this course should only be pursued at the express instructions of the family. Paying taxes or giving to charity should
be a *conscious choice* after the family is given enough information to choose taxes over a complex plan.

One of the primary reasons for failure to implement a
comprehensive wealth transfer plan is that the senior generation often lacks a real understanding of what it is they
want to accomplish. Without strong commitment to an
end goal, people will not usually be willing to give the extra
effort and expense necessary to complete such a plan. Tax
savings alone are rarely sufficient motivation. Professionals
working together with affluent families can help these families better identify their real dreams. Then, using the ideas
contained in these pages and the simplified explanation of
the various tools, the team can design and build a wall
around the family's wealth.

Appendix A

The Four Tier Accounting System

Split interest charitable trusts have a unique set of accounting rules that are important from both design and investment perspectives. The uses and benefits of a charitable remainder trust cannot be fully explored without a basic understanding of these rules. The basic rule is sometimes called "WIFO," or worst-in-first-out. The four tiers are: ordinary income, capital gain, tax-exempt, and principal.

When an asset is contributed to a CRT it becomes the principal of the trust in the top tier of the trust. The basis of the asset is the same as it was in the hands of the donor. Once the asset is sold, the gain realized on the sale creates capital gain (assuming the asset is a capital asset) and the original basis remains in the top tier as principal, while the gain drops down to tier two as capital gain. If the trustee were to keep the proceeds temporarily in cash (earning no interest), the payout to the income beneficiaries would still be taxed as capital gain, even though reducing the original asset base. Once gain is realized by the trust, no distributions will be treated as tax exempt or a return of principal until the capital gain tier is reduced to zero. It is as if the lower tiers contained dyes that colored the money that flowed down from the upper tiers.

Once the proceeds from the sale of the original assets are reinvested, the character of the profits from the ongoing investments are added to their respective tiers and the distributions are taxed accordingly. For example, if a standard CRT with an 8 percent payout earned 12 percent in its first year of operation, with 3 percent being dividends or interest and 9 percent being long term capital gain, the income recipients' 8 percent payment will be reported as 3 percent ordinary income and 5 percent long term capital gain. The 4 percent total return (we will assume it was all realized gains) above the payout rate will be retained by the trust in tier two as additional long term capital gain, but the trust would pay no tax on the 4 percent excess.

If in the following year the trust had no ordinary income and no capital gain (assume it took the money and put it in a checking account with no interest), the 8 percent payment would be characterized as all long term capital gain. The first 4 percent of the payment would essentially be from the excess 4 percent return in year one. The balance would reduce the tier to retained capital gains from the sale of the originally contributed asset. All current and accumulated tier one and tier two income must be paid out before any tax-exempt income in tier three can be accessed as exempt income. Some advisers mistakenly believe that one can sell an appreciated asset in a CRT, invest in municipal bonds, and receive tax-free income. This is not so.

However, there is an occasional planning opportunity here. With capital gains rates at 20 percent (federal only), and relatively tight spreads between some municipal bonds and treasuries, a CRT portfolio investing in munis could allow an income recipient to pay 20 percent on the interest from those bonds and have more net income than after paying 39.6 percent on treasury bonds.

Appendix B

Court Cases

This appendix contains the text of some of the landmark cases in the wealth transfer planning areas. The author decided to include them because they are very important for professionals and those interested in better understanding the cases that most affect key areas of estate and charitable planning.

Palmer v. Commissioner, 62 T.C. 684

DANIEL D. PALMER AND AGNES H. PALMER, PETITIONERS v. COMMISSIONER OF INTERNAL REVENUE, RESPONDENT

Docket No. 2557-71.   Filed August 27, 1974.

1. Palmer College was owned and operated by a profit-making corporation. The assets of the college comprised approximately 80 percent of the assets of the corporation. Approximately 70 percent of the outstanding shares of the

corporation stock was owned by a trust of which the petitioner was trustee and Income beneficiary. The remaining shares were owned outright by the petitioner. On Aug. 31, 1966, a charitable organization, of which the petitioner was controlling trustee, purchased the shares owned by the trust. On the same day, the petitioner contributed enough shares to the foundation so that It thereafter owned 80 percent of the outstanding shares. On the next day, the corporation redeemed all the shares held by the foundation in return for the college assets. Held, in substance and form, the contribution was of stock and not the proceeds of the redemption.

2. In 1961, the estate of the petitioner's father demanded that the Corporation redeem shares of its stock in accordance with an agreement between the petitioner's father and the corporation which set forth the formula for determining the redemption price. In 1964, after vigorous negotiations concerning the validity of the agreement, the stock was redeemed. Held, the corporation was not a willing buyer of the stock, and therefore, the redemption is not a comparable sale from which the fair market value of the stock in 1966 can be determined.

SIMPSON, Judge: The respondent determined a deficiency of $178,309.72 in the Federal income tax of the petitioners for the year 1966. Two issues are presented for decision. The first is whether in substance, as well as in form, a contribution of stock by the petitioners preceded the redemption of such stock, when the redemption took place the very next day. In the event we find that the contribution, in substance, preceded the redemption, we must determine whether the fair market value of the stock was less than claimed by the petitioners in their return.

FINDINGS OF FACT

Some of the facts have been stipulated, and those facts are so found.

Upon the death of the petitioner's grandfather, the petitioner's father, Dr. Bartlett Joshua (B.J.) Palmer, suc-

ceeded to the presidency of the college and the corporation.
On November 7, 1959, an agreement between the corporation and Dr. B. J. Palmer was executed. That agreement
granted cross-options to his estate (the estate) and the corporation — the estate could require that the corporation
purchase all its stock in the corporation, and the corporation
could require that the estate sell all of such stock to it. The
purchase price for such sale was to be the book value of the
shares as of the last day of the month preceding the month
in which Dr. B. J. Palmer died.

The petitioner's father died in May 1961, and the rela-
tionships which developed between the petitioner and the
executors of the estate were marked by disagreement, hostil-
ity, and ill will.

A recitation in the will of Dr. B. J. Palmer stated that
he and his wife had amply endowed their son during their
lifetimes, and therefore, no provision was made for the petitioner. As a result, the petitioner brought a legal action
against the executors and trustees to invalidate his father's
will. Judgment was entered for the estate, an appeal was
taken, and the Supreme Court of Iowa affirmed. Palmer v.
Evans, 255 Iowa 1176, 124 N.W. 2d 856 (1963).

As early as before the death of his father, the petitioner
contemplated the possibility of making the college into a
nonprofit institution. It was felt that alumni financial support in the form of gifts and bequests was being withheld
principally because would-be donors were reluctant to contribute and thereby enrich the holdings of the Palmer family. In addition, it was felt that contributions were not made
because they were not deductible for purposes of the Federal
income and estate taxes, and that participation in certain
Federal funding programs was denied the college because it
was not a nonprofit institution. Moreover, because the corporation was operated for profit, graduates of the college
encountered difficulty obtaining licenses to practice chiropractic in at least one State. Accordingly, the petitioner
caused the Palmer College Foundation (the foundation) to

be organized in 1964 as a corporation not for pecuniary profit.

In general, the foundation was organized to engage in religious, charitable, educational, and scientific activities. Specifically, it was intended and empowered to take over ownership of the college from the corporation. In addition, the foundation was empowered to accept gifts, to make loans to students, and to award scholarships, research grants, and prizes for meritorious essays.

During the entire year in issue, 1966, the certificates were held as specified in the bylaws. As a result, the petitioner controlled the foundation. Not only was he the controlling trustee by virtue of having personal control over the majority of the certificates, but he was also its president and a director. Moreover, Mrs. Palmer was a trustee and director, and the other directors and officers of the foundation were personally chosen by the petitioner and were the same individuals as the officers and directors of the corporation.

In 1966, the corporation had outstanding 2,896.97 shares of common stock, par value $100, prior to September 1 of that year. Of the shares, 2,078.97 shares were owned by a trust (the trust) created under the last will and testament (the will) of Mabel H. Palmer, the petitioner's mother, and the remaining 818 shares were owned by the petitioner. Under the terms of the will, the petitioner was trustee and income beneficiary of the trust, Mrs. Agnes H. Palmer was a contingent income beneficiary, and the three minor daughters of the petitioner were the ultimate remaindermen.

The petitioner exercised effective control of the corporation and the college throughout 1966. Prior to September 1, 1966, he was president of the college, president of the corporation, and a member of the latter's board of directors. Of the three other officers of the corporation at that time, two were close friends and longtime associates of the petitioner, and of such three officers, two were directors.

The petitioner, as president of the corporation, was actively engaged in the operations of the college. One of his major concerns was the continuation of the pure essence of chiropractic as taught by his grandfather and father, and the petitioner had the final say with respect to curriculum selection, employment and assignment of the faculty, and other staff and budgetary considerations. In addition, he was involved in fund-raising activities among alumni.

The petitioner engaged counsel to devise a plan that would accomplish the transfer the college from the corporation to the foundation, that would enable the petitioner to maintain his control over the direction and operation of the college, and that would yield the most favorable tax consequences. In connection with the development of such plan, a local real estate appraiser was engaged to value the land and improvements owned by the corporation. His conclusions on valuation were summarized in a covering letter dated September 14, 1965, which was addressed to the treasurer of the corporation and attached to his appraisal report. In that letter, he determined the fair market value of the college assets appraised by him was $2 million.

Next, a national accounting firm was employed, in part, for the purpose of making a pro forma allocation of corporate assets between those relating to the educational facilities to be transferred to the foundation and the other assets to be retained by the corporation. Using information provided by the treasurer of the corporation, the accounting firm allocated $776,744.85 to the corporation and $2,468,827.35 to the foundation.

On August 31, 1966, the foundation acquired the shares of stock in the corporation held by the trust in return for a promissory note in the face amount of $1,794,000. The purchase price, which amounted to $863 per share, was determined on the basis of the aforementioned appraisal of the real estate owned by the corporation, an estimate concerning the value of the name and goodwill of the college, and the book value of its other assets and liabilities. Under the terms of the promissory note, the principal was payable in annual installments of $51,257 over a 35-year period, with the final payment being somewhat larger in amount. Simple interest at the rate of 4 percent per annum was payable upon each installment. No downpayment was required.

Prior to the purchase of the stock from the trust, the foundation did not have assets with which to pay the promissory note. In its application for exemption in the year 1964, the foundation listed its current assets as $4,246.90, and for the period ending December 31, 1965, it reported total assets of $37,087.50. It was intended that the foundation would obtain the funds necessary for payment of the installment obligations primarily from the operations of the college.

Also on August 31, 1966, the petitioner transferred 238 shares of stock of the corporation to the foundation. Thereafter, the foundation owned 2,316.97 shares, which represented 79.979 percent of the total issued and outstanding shares of the corporation. The parties have treated such amount as 80 percent, and so shall we.

At the meeting in which the board of directors and trustees of the foundation authorized the purchase of stock from the trust, it was resolved that the foundation, as owner of in excess of 70 percent of the stock of the corporation, would convene a joint directors and stockholders meeting, for the purpose of considering the redemption of the stock held by the foundation. In addition, the board of directors and the trustees were authorized to effectuate the redemption.

At 10 o'clock in the morning of the next day, September 1, 1966, the board of directors and shareholders of the corporation met and approved an agreement whereby the shares of the corporation stock held by the foundation were to be redeemed in return for the operating assets of the college. At 2 o'clock in the afternoon of the same day, the board of directors and trustees of the foundation met specially to consider and approve that redemption. All these meetings took place in the administration building of the college.

After the performance of the redemption agreement of September 1, 1966, all of the operating assets of the college were owned directly by the foundation, and the primary business of the corporation became the ownership, leasing, and sale of real property. After such transfer, the petitioner exercised the same degree of control over the direction and administration of the college as he did when the college was operated by the corporation.

In his return for the year 1966, the petitioner claimed a charitable deduction of $52,640.72 attributable to the transfer of 238 shares of stock of the corporation to the foundation. The stock was treated as having a value of $863 per share. In his notice of deficiency, the respondent determined that the contribution of stock followed by its redemption was in substance a distribution to the petitioner essentially equivalent to a dividend, and determined that the amount of such distribution was $205,394, the value of the assets represented by such stock. He also determined that the petitioner's charitable contribution deduction should be increased by $62,706.40 as a result of the increase in his gross income. In an amended answer, the respondent determined that the entire deduction for the charitable contribution should be disallowed.

OPINION

The respondent has challenged the gift of stock to the foundation. He claims that the ultimate objective of the petitioner was to bring about a transfer of assets to the foundation and that the gift of stock was meaningless. In support of that contention, the respondent argues that the gift was illusory, incomplete, and transitory, and that in any event, it should be disregarded as an intermediary step of a single, integrated transaction. If not disregarded, the gift by the petitioner was, according to the respondent, an anticipatory assignment of the proceeds of the redemption which would otherwise be taxable to the petitioner as a distribution under sections 302 and 301. Finally, the respondent challenged the deduction on the grounds that the stock was worth a great deal less than that claimed by the petitioner.

Section 170 allows a deduction for any charitable contribution made during the taxable year. If we find that in fact the petitioner did make a contribution of the 238 shares in 1966, he is entitled to deduct the fair market value of such contribution, subject to the percentage limitations on such a deduction. However, if we were to find that the petitioner arranged for a redemption of such shares and then contributed the assets so acquired to the foundation, the tax consequences would be significantly different. Under section 302, the amounts distributed to a shareholder in redemption of his stock may be taxed to him as a dividend under section 301 or may be treated as the proceeds of the sale of a capital asset. In either event, the petitioner would most likely be taxable on some income as a result of the redemption, but he would be allowed a charitable contribution deduction with respect to the value of the assets contributed to the foundation. Thus, the heart of the controversy is whether the petitioner is taxable on any income as a result of the series of transactions which took place on August 31 and September 1, 1966.

In Humacid Co., 42 T.C. 894, 913 (1964), we said:

The law with respect to gifts appreciated property is well established. A gift of appreciated property does not result in income to the donor so long as he gives the property away absolutely and parts with title thereto before the property gives rise to income by way of a sale.

Carrington v. Commissioner, 476 F.2d 704 (C.A. 5, 1973), affirming a Memorandum Opinion of this Court; Behrend v. United States, and unreported case (C.A. 4, 1972, 31 A.F.T.R. 2d 73-406, 73-1 U.S.T.C. par. 9123); DeWitt v. United States, 503 F.2d 1406 (Ct. Cl. 1974); Sheppard v. United States, 361 F.2d 972 (Ct. Cl. 1966); Winton v. Kelm, 122 F. Supp. 649 (D. Minn. 1954); Apt v. Birmingham, 89 F. Supp. 361 (N.D. Iowa 1950).

However, the respondent contended that such principles of law are not applicable in this case and presented a variety of arguments in support of his position. He urged that tax consequences are determined on the basis of the substance of the transaction, and not its form, and that because the petitioner conceived the plan for the transfer of the college to the foundation and controlled all parties to that transfer, there was, in substance, no gift of stock to the foundation. He invoked the step-transaction doctrine and suggested that since the various steps toward the accomplishment of the petitioner's objective were interdependent, they should be ignored for tax purposes. Finally, he asserted that the petitioner had the power to bring about a redemption of his stock and that, therefore, there was in effect merely an assignment of income by him.

The principles urged by the respondent are sound and well established in our tax law. The incidence of taxation depends upon the substance of the transaction and not mere formalism. Commissioner v. Court Holding Co., 324 U.S. 331, 334 (1945). Taxation is not so much concerned with refinements of title as it is with actual command over the property. Corliss v. Bowers, 281 U.S. 376, 378 (1930); see also Commissioner v. P. G. Lake, Inc., 356 U.S. 260 (1958); Helvering v. Clifford, 309 U.S. 331 (1940); Griffiths v. Commissioner, 308 U.S. 355 (1939); Sachs v. Commissioner, 277 F.2d 879, 882-883 (C.A. 8, 1960), affirming 32 T.C. 815 (1959). Under such cases, a mere transfer in form, without substance, may be disregarded for tax purposes. Commissioner v. P.G. Lake, Inc., supra; Commissioner v. Court Holding Co., supra; Commissioner v. Sunnen, 333 U.S. 591 (1948); Helvering v. Clifford, supra; Corliss v. Bowers, supra; Richardson v. Smith,, 102 F.2d 697 (C.A. 2, 1939); Howard Cook, 5 T.C. 908 (1945); J.L. McInerney, 29 B.T.A. 1 (1933), affd. 82 F.2d 665 ((C.A. 6, 1936).

As a corollary to the general proposition of those cases, it has been stated by the Supreme Court that "A given result at the end of a straight path is not made a different result because reached by following a devious path." Minnesota

Tea Co. v. Helvering, 302 U.S. 609, 613 (1938). Accordingly, where a taxpayer has embarked on a series of transactions that are in substance a single, unitary, or indivisible transaction, the courts have disregarded the intermediary steps and have given credence only to the completed transaction. E.g., Redwing Carriers, Inc. v. Tomlinson, 399 F.2d 652, 654 (C.A. 5, 1968); May Broadcasting Co. v. United States, 200 F.2d 852 (C.A. 8, 1953); Whitney Corporation v. Commissioner, 105 F.2d 438 (C.A. 8, 1939), affirming 38 B.T.A. 224 (1938); Commissioner v. Ashland Oil & R. Co., 99 F.2d 588 (C.A. 6 1938), reversing sub nom. Swiss Oil Corporation, 32 B.T.A. 777 (1935), certiorari denied 306 U.S. 661 (1939); James Kuper, 61 T.C. 624 (1974); Kimbell-Diamond Millig Co., 14 T.C. 74 (1950), affirmed per curiam 187 F.2d 718 (C.A. 5, 1951), certiorari denied 342 U.S. 827 (1951). Transactions that are challenged as intermediary steps of an integrated transaction are disregarded only when found to be so interdependent that the legal relations created by one transaction would have been fruitless without the completion of the series. American Bantam Car Co., 11 T.C. 397, 405 (1948), affd. 177 F.2d 513 (C.A. 3, 1949), certiorari denied 339 U.S. 920 (1950); see Scientific Instrument Co., 17 T.C. 1253 (1952), affirmed per curiam 202 F.2d 155 (C.A. 6, 1953).

As a general rule, a taxpayer cannot insulate himself from taxation merely by assigning a right to income to another. Commissioner v. Sunnen, supra; Helvering v. Horst, 311 U.S. 112 (1940); Corliss v. Bowers, supra; Lucas v. Earl, 281 U.S. 111 (1930). If the putative assignor performs services (Lucas v. Earl), retains the property (Helvering v. Horst), or retains the control over the use and enjoyment of the income (Commissioner v. Sunnen; Corliss v. Bowers), the liability for the tax remains on his shoulders. However, if the entire interest in the property is transferred and the assignor retains no incidence of either direct or indirect control, then the tax on the income rests on the assignee. Blair v. Commissioner, 300 U.S. 5 (1937);

Carrington v. Commissioner, supra; Behrend v. United States, supra; DeWitt v. United States, supra; Humacid Co., 42 T.C. 894 (1964); Winton v. Kelm, supra; Apt v. Birmingham, supra.

Despite the undoubted validity of those doctrines, we find them to be inapplicable in this case. Similar attacks have been presented by the respondent in a variety of cases involving gifts of stock followed by its redemption, and the attacks have generally been rejected by the courts. Grove v. Commissioner 490 F.2d 241 (C.A. 2, 1973), affirming a Memorandum Opinion of this Court; Carrington v. Commissioner, 476 F.2d 704 (C.A. 5, 1973); Behrend v. United States, an unreported Case ((C.A. 4, 1972, 31 A.F.T.R. 2d 73-406, 73-1 U.S.T.C. par. 9123); DeWitt v. United States, 503 F.2d 1406 (Ct. Cl. 1974); Sheppard v. United States, 361 F.2d 972 (Ct. Cl. 1966); Winton v. Kelm, 122 F. Supp. 649 (D. Minn. 1954); Apt v. Birmingham, 89 F. Supp. 361 (N.D. Iowa 1950); see Humacid Co., supra. The petitioner wished to have the college become a non-profit organization, and there were two paths which he could have taken — he could have had the stock redeemed and then made a contribution of the assets, or he could have contributed the stock and let the donee arrange for the redemption. The tax consequences to the donor turn on which path he chooses, and so long as there is substance to what he does, there is no requirement that he choose the more expensive way. Gregory v. Helvering, 293 U.S. 465 (1935). He arranged for the transfer to precede the redemption, and there is no reason for us to conclude that such a sequence of events lacked any more substance than for the redemption to precede the transfer, as suggested by the respondent. Carrington v. Commissioner, 476 F.2d at 706. The only question is whether he really made a gift, thereby transferring ownership of the stock prior to the redemption.

Even though the donor anticipated or was aware that the redemption was imminent, the presence of an actual gift and the absence of an obligation to have the stock

redeemed have been sufficient to give such gifts indepen-
dent significance. (Emphasis added.) Carrington v.
Commissioner, supra; DeWitt v. United States, supra;
Sheppard v. United States, supra. It is true that the petitioner controlled the foundation. However, the foundation
was a charitable organization that was organized for certain
specific purposes. Under Iowa law, the petitioner was subject to the responsibilities and duties of a fiduciary when he
acted as director and trustee of the foundation (Schildberg
Rock Products Co. v. Brooks, 258 Iowa 759, 140 N.W. 2d
132, 136-137 (1966); Des Moines Bank & Trust Co. v.
George M. Bechtel & Co., 243 Iowa 1007, 51 N.W. 2d 174,
215-217 (1952)), and there is nothing in the record to indicate that he exercised command over the use and enjoyment of property of the foundation in violation of his fiduciary duty. There has been no allegation or evidence that
the foundation was a sham. In these circumstances, it
appears clear that the foundation was not an alter ego of the
petitioner, and in fact it had dominion and control over the
shares of stock received by gift from the petitioner, notwithstanding the fact that the petitioner was the controlling
trustee. United States v. Morss, 159 F.2d 142 (C.A. 1,
1947); Theodore D. Stern, 15 T.C. 521 (1950); Crosby v.
United States, an unreported case (S.D. Miss. 1973, 31
A.F.T.R. 2d 73-1191, 73-1 U.S.T.C. par. 9399); Winton v.
Kelm, supra; see William Waller, 39 T.C. 665 (1963).

Although, after the gift and the redemption, the petitioner retained power and control over the curriculum and
policies of the college, such control was not tantamount to
the control and dominion of an owner over the use and
enjoyment of property. His control of the affairs of the college was akin to the manager of a business, but he had no
right to share in its profits. In an analogous situation involving a gift to a family member of a partnership interest to be
held in trust, retention by the donor of the control of the
business was not sufficient reason, alone, to restructure the
gift and the resulting interest in the profits of the partner-

ship. Kuney v. United States, 448 F.2d 22 ((C.A. 9, 1971);
Theodore D. Stern, supra; Edward D. Sultan, 18 T.C. 715
(1952), affirmed per curiam 210 F.2d 652 (C.A. 9, 1954);
compare Commissioner v. Sunnen, 333 U.S. 591 (1948). In
Behrend v. United States, supra, the donor's control over
the charity and the corporation was not sufficient to cause
the restructure of the gift and the redemption of the stock
there in issue. There is no discernible difference between the
facts of that case and those before us.

In Hudspeth v. United States, 471 F.2d 275 (C.A. 8,
1972), the taxpayer owned 80 percent of the stock in a closely held, family-owned corporation. In April 1964, the directors adopted and the shareholders ratified a plan of complete
liquidation. Before the corporation filed articles of dissolution with the proper State authority and before the assets
were distributed to the shareholders, the taxpayer donated
67 shares, or less than 7 percent, of the stock to a charity.
Regardless of that transfer, the court held that in substance,
the taxpayer transferred the proceeds of dissolution. Under
the court's reasoning, it was significant that the gift was
made after the vote for liquidation. That vote signified the
taxpayer's intent to convert the corporation into the essential elements of his investment. Moreover, the donee was
powerless to reverse or have revoked the decision to liquidate. See John P. Kinsey, 58 T.C. 259 (1972), affd. 477 F.2d
1058 (C.A. 2, 1973); Howard Cook, 5 T.C. 908 (1945). The
court considered that those facts made the case distinguishable from cases in which either no plan had been adopted at
the time of the gift even though liquidation was anticipated
and planned (e.g., Winton v. Kelm, supra; Apt v. Birmingham, supra), or the donee was given sufficient interest to
reverse the decision to liquidate (e.g., W. B. Rushing, 52
T.C. 888 (1969), affd. 441 F.2d 593 (C.A. 5, 1971)).

In our opinion, the facts herein are more akin to those
in W. B. Rushing, supra, Winton v. Kelm, supra, and Apt v.
Birmingham, supra, and are distinguishable from those in
Hudspeth v. United States, supra, John P. Kinsey, supra, and

Howard Cook, supra. When the foundation received the gift of stock from the petitioner, no vote for the redemption had yet been taken. Although we recognize that the vote was anticipated, nonetheless, under the Hudspeth reasoning, that expectation is not enough. We have found that the foundation was not a sham, was not an alter-ego of the petitioner, and that it received his entire interest in the 238 shares of the corporation stock. On the same day, it acquired enough shares of stock from the trust to hold in the aggregate 80 percent of the outstanding shares of the corporation. Thereafter, the foundation voted for the redemption. It did so because the redemption was in its interest. At the time of the gift, that vote had not yet been taken, and by the afternoon of August 31, 1966, the foundation had the voting power to prevent the redemption, if it wished to do so. In these circumstances, at the time of the gift, the redemption had not proceeded far enough along for us to conclude that the foundation was powerless to reverse the plans of the petitioner. In light of the presence of an actual, valid gift and because the foundation was not a sham, we hold that the gift of stock was not in substance a gift of the proceeds of redemption.

Decision will be entered for the petitioners.

Notes

1. All statutory references are to the Internal Revenue Code for 1954, unless otherwise indicated.
2. In the Tax Reform Act of 1969, Congress dealt with contributions of income and appreciated property, and by the enactment of sec. 170(e), it modified the law applicable gifts made after 1969. See sec. 170(e), and sec. 1.170A-4, Income Tax Regs.
3. See also Robert L. Fox, 37 P.-H. Memo. T.C. par. 68,205,27 T.C.M. 1001 (1968); but see Russell E. Phelon, 35 P.-H. Memo. T.C. par. 66,199,25 T.C.M. 1024 (1966).

Estate Of Daniel J. Harrison, Jr., Deceased, Daniel J. Harrison III And Bruce F. Harrison, Independent Co-Executors V. Commissioner.

T.C. Memo 1987–8

Docket No. 19980-84.   Filed January 6, 1987.

J. Thomas Eubank, S. Stacy Eastland, and Charles A. Crocker, for the petitioner.

David W. Johnson, for the respondent.

MEMORANDUM OPINION

SHIELDS, Judge: Respondent determined a deficiency of $31,758,893.37 in the estate tax due from the Estate of Daniel J. Harrison, Jr. After concessions, these issues remain for decision: (1) the value for estate tax purposes of a limited partnership interest owned by decedent; (2) whether the estate is entitled to a deduction under section 2053 for estimated interest on installment payments of the estate tax due respondent and the inheritance tax due the State of Texas; and (3) whether petitioner is entitled to a deduction under section 2053 for post-death interest paid by the estate on a debt incurred by decedent during his lifetime.

The facts in this case were fully stipulated. The stipulation of facts and attached exhibits are incorporated herein by reference.

Petitioner is the estate of Daniel J. Harrison, Jr. ("decedent") who died at the age of 60 on January 14, 1980, a resident of Houston Texas. The independent co-executors of the estate are Daniel J. Harrison III ("Dan") and Bruce F. Harrison ("Bruce"), the sons of decedent. They were also residents of Houston, Texas at the time the petition was filed.

Limited Partnership Interest. On June 10, 1975, decedent, whose health was declining, executed a power of attorney generally authorizing Dan to manage his assets which included extensive ranching properties and other real estate as well as oil and gas interests in both developed and undeveloped properties. Decedent's health continued to decline and Dan continued to manage his father's properties under the power of attorney until August 1, 1979. On that date Bruce and Dan, acting individually and under the power of attorney for the decedent, organized Harrison Interests, Ltd., a Texas limited partnership, with the principal purpose of consolidating and preserving decedent's assets. On the same date, Dan, under the power of attorney for decedent, contributed assets of the decedent to the partnership in return for a 1 percent general partnership interest and a 77.8 percent limited partnership interest.

At the same time Dan and Bruce also contributed assets to the partnership in return for separate 10.6 percent general partnership interests. The assets contributed by each of the partners consisted primarily of real estate, oil and gas interests, and marketable securities that the decedent and his sons had accumulated. None of the properties contributed to the partnership by either Dan or Bruce had been given to them by decedent.

The combined value of decedent's general partnership interest and his limited partnership interest at the time of the creation of the partnership was $59,476,523, which was the value of the properties contributed by decedent to the partnership. Dan's general partnership interest and Bruce's general partnership interest each had a value at the creation of the partnership of $7,981,351, which was the value of the assets they each contributed to the partnership.

Under the partnership agreement, the general partners had absolute control over the management of the partnership. Each general partner also had the right during life to dissolve the partnership, but neither a limited partner nor a successor to a general partner had such a right. The partnership agreement provided that the partnership was to be automatically dissolved upon the death of a general partner, or upon an election to dissolve by a living general partner, unless within 90 days of such death, or such election, all of the other general partners agreed to continue the partnership. In such case, the partnership was to continue, but the estate of the deceased general partner, or the living general partner electing to dissolve the partnership, was entitled to a payment equal to the amount he would have received had the partnership been dissolved.

Under the partnership agreement, both general partners and limited partners had the right to sell or assign their partnership interests after first giving the other general partners an option to buy such interests. Similarly, the agreement also provided that upon the death of a general partner, his legal representative was required to give the remaining general partners an option to buy the deceased partner's general partnership interest.

On January 14, 1980, decedent died of another stroke. On February 4, 1980, Dan and Bruce exercised their option to purchase decedent's general partnership interest for $757,116. This sale was confirmed by a decree of a probate court for Harris County, Texas, on March 12, 1980. Pursuant to the partnership agreement, Dan and Bruce also agreed within ninety days after decedent's death to continue the partnership.

In this case, respondent and petitioner agree that $757,116 is the value of decedent's general partnership interest. They disagree, however, as to the value of his limited partnership interest. Respondent claims that the value of the limited partnership interest is $59,555,020, which is the agreed value of the proportionate share of the partnership assets that decedent would have received for his limited partnership interest if the partnership had been dissolved or if decedent's limited partnership interest had been terminated immediately before his death pursuant to the partnership agreement. Petitioner contends that the value of the limited partnership interest is $33,000,000 which we find from the stipulation of the parties was the value of the limited partnership interest the moment after it passed from the decedent to his estate. The difference between the two values is attributable entirely to the right which decedent had as a general partner up until his death to force a dissolution of the partnership.

The parties agree that under the partnership agreement and applicable Texas law this right did not pass to the estate.

Respondent relies on sections 2033, 2035, 2036, 2037, 2038, and 2041 in support of his argument that the value of decedent's limited partnership interest for estate tax purposes is $59,555,020, the amount at which he could have forced its liquidation immediately before his death.

Respondent's reliance upon sections 2033 is inapposite, however, as is well illustrated by the reasoning in United States v. Land, 303 F.2d 170, 171-173 (5th Cir. 1962), cert. denied 371 U.S. 862 (1962), where it was stated:

The statute applicable here is *** Section 2033 of the Internal Revenue Code ***. This provides that "the gross estate shall include the value of all property *** to the extent of the interest therein of the decedent at the time of his death." The Regulations reiterate the truism that the tax is "an excise tax on the transfer of property at death and is not a tax on the property transferred." Treas. Reg. 20.2033-1(a). It is of course imperative that the tax be imposed on the TRANSFER of the property in order to avoid the constitutional prohibition against unapportioned direct taxes. From this *** it follows that the valuation of the estate should be made at the time of the transfer. The time of transfer is the time of death. Treas. Reg. 20.2031-1(b). In Knowlton v. Moore, 1900, 178 U.S. 41, 56, 20 S. Ct. 747, 44 L. Ed. 969 the Supreme Court said, "tax laws of this nature in all countries rest in their essence upon the principle that death is the generating source from which the particular taxing power takes its being and that it is the power to transmit, or the transmission from the dead to the living, on which such taxes are more immediately rested." [Emphasis supplied; citations omitted.]

Brief as is the instant of death, the court must pinpoint its valuation at this instant — the moment of truth, when the ownership of the decedent ends and the ownership of the successor begins. It is a fallacy, therefore, to argue value before — or — after death on the notion that valuation must be determined by the value either of the interest that ceases or of the interest that begins. INSTEAD, THE VAL-UATION IS DETERMINED BY THE INTEREST THAT PASSES AND THE VALUE OF THE INTEREST BE-FORE OR AFTER DEATH IS PERTINENT ONLY AS IT SERVES TO INDICATE THE VALUE AT DEATH. In the usual case death brings no change in the value of prop-erty. It is only in the few cases where death alters value, as well as ownership, that it is necessary to determine whether the value at the time of death reflects the change caused by death, for example, loss of services of a valuable partner to a small business. [Emphasis added.]

*   *   *   *   *   *

Underlying the determination in these instances that the valuation of property passing at death reflects the changes wrought by death is a basic economic fact: value looks ahead. To find the fair market value of a Property interest at the decedent's death we put ourselves in the posi-tion of a potential purchaser of the interest at that time. Such a person would Not be influenced in his calculations by past risks that had failed to materialize or by restrictions that had ended. Death tolls the bell for risks, contingencies, or restrictions which exist only during the life of the dece-dent. A potential buyer focuses on the value the property has in the present or will have in the future. He attributes full value to any right that vests or matures at death, and he reduces his valuation to account for any risk or deprivation that death brings into effect, such as the effect of the death on the brains of a small, close corporation. These are factors that would affect his enjoyment of the property should he purchase it, and on which he bases his valuation. The sense of the situation suggests that we follow suit. [Emphasis added.]

When the foregoing reasoning is applied to this case, it is apparent that the property transferred at the moment of decedent's death was the limited partnership interest that passed to decedent's estate, which did not include the right to dissolve the partnership. Nevertheless, respondent claims that when decedent's right to dissolve the partnership terminated at his death something of value passed to Dan and Bruce. However, we are unable to agree because this contention is contrary to respondent's stipulation that the value of the interests of Dan and Bruce were the same at the moment before decedent's death, at the moment of decedent's death, and at the moment after decedent's death.

Respondent also contends that we should ignore the effect the partnership agreement has upon decedent's limited partnership interest because the partnership agreement was an attempt to artificially depress the value of decedent's property for estate tax purposes. Such an agreement will be ignored only if there is no business purpose for the creation of the partnership or if the agreement is merely a substitute for testamentary disposition. See Estate of Bischoff v. Commissioner, 69 T.C. 32, 39-41 (1977).

With respect to business purpose, petitioner presented convincing proof that the partnership was created as a means of providing necessary and proper management of decedent's properties and that the partnership was advantageous to and in the best interests of decedent. Respondent presented no proof to rebut petitioner's showing.

With respect to the issue of whether the agreement was a substitute for testamentary disposition, we find in petitioner's favor for three reasons. First, the agreement applied to all the partners, and no partner's assignee or estate could liquidate the partnership without the remaining partners' consent. See Estate of Bischoff, 69 T.C. at 41;

Estate of Littick v. Commissioner, 31 T.C. 181, 186-188 (1958). Furthermore, decedent received adequate consideration for his transfer to the partnership. See Estate of Bischoff, 69 T.C. at 41 n. 9. Finally, although the creation of the partnership eventually resulted in a substantial decrease in estate taxes, there is no proof in the record that the partnership was created other than for business purposes.

Having determined that the property interest to be valued is that which passed to the decedent's estate, we must now decide how to value it. As stated in United States v. Land, supra, we must pinpoint our valuation at the instant of death, "the moment of truth, when the ownership of the decedent ends and the ownership of the successor begins." 303 F.2d at 172. The value thus pinpointed is to be determined by reference to the classical fair market value, the amount at which the limited partnership interest would have changed hands between a willing seller and a willing buyer with neither being under any compulsion and both having reasonable knowledge of the relevant circumstances. Section 2031; section 20.2031(b), Estate Tax Regs. As also noted in Land, a potential buyer of the partnership interest would focus on the value of such interest in the present or the future, not the past. Thus, decedent's right during life to liquidate the partnership would no longer be available to enhance the value of the partnership interest after his death. Put simply the only purchase available to such a potential buyer in this case would be the limited partnership interest without any right to liquidate the partnership. As previously indicated, the parties have stipulated that the value of such interest is $33,000,000.

Respondent next contends that under section 2035 the gross estate includes the right to liquidate the partnership as property transferred by the decedent witout adequate and full consideration during the three-year period ending on his death. In this connection, respondent argues that when the decedent originally transferred his assets to the partnership he failed to retain for his estate the right to liquidate the partnership while the other partners retained such right for their estates. Thus, according to respondent, decedent transferred without adequate consideration and in contemplation of death something of value to the other partners when the partnership was created. We disagree because we find that Dan and Bruce did not retain a liquidation right for their estates since, in this respect, the partnership agreement treats all three partners equally. Furthermore, as stipulated to by respondent, the decedent received partnership interests equal in value to the assets he contributed to the partnership, thus, there was adequate and full consideration for his transfer. Moreover, no transfer was made by decedent to Dan and Bruce since they received partnership interests having stipulated values equal to the assets they contributed to the partnership.

Respondent also contends that under section 2036 the gross estate includes the right to liquidate the partnership as property transferred by the decedent without adequate consideration and over which he retained for his life the right to possession, enjoyment, or the income therefrom. As noted above, decedent's transfer to the partnership was for a full and adequate consideration. In addition, he retained no rights in the transferred property, but instead acquired partnership interests having equal value.

We are also unable to agree with respondent's contention that the decedent's estate includes the right to liquidate the partnership under section 2037 as property transferred by the decedent without adequate consideration where he retained a reversionary interest in the property and the enjoyment of the property could be obtained only by surviving the decedent. Here again, this section is not applicable because there was adequate and full consideration given for decedent's transfer. Furthermore, he did not retain a reversionary interest in the assets, and the enjoyment of the other partners of their interest in the assets contributed by him to the partnership was not postponed until the death of decedent.

Section 2038 is equally inapplicable because there was no gratuitous transfer by the decedent and he retained no right to alter or terminate the transfer to the partnership.

Section 2041 is inapplicable because decedent did not retain a general power of appointment over the property transferred to the partnership.

In conclusion, given the facts stipulated to by respondent and the absence of any proof putting into question the purpose of the partnership, we hold that for estate tax purposes the value of the decedent's limited partnership interest was $33,000,000.

Estimated Interest Expense on Estate and Inheritance Taxes. In the estate tax return, petitioner elected under section 6166 to pay the estate tax in ten equal annual installments. Respondent approved the election. Petitioner also deferred payment of a portion of the inheritance tax due the State of Texas.

At the date of trial, petitioner had paid interest of $4,782,324 to respondent on the estate tax. Petitioner also had paid interest on the inheritance tax in the amount of $624,137. Respondent agrees that these amounts plus any such interest which is paid by petitioner prior to the decision being entered in this case qualify for deduction from the gross estate under section 2053(a)(2).

Respondent, however, does not agree that petitioner is entitled to deduct interest not paid as of the date of this decision but estimated to be paid by the date of the last installment of the estate and inheritance taxes. Petitioner has estimated, using a 12 percent interest rate, that interest yet to be paid on the estate tax is $5,244,715, and interest yet to be paid on the inheritance tax is $49,114.

In Estate of Bailly v. Commissioner, 81 T.C. 246, modified, 81 T.C. 949 (1983), we concluded that interest on state inheritance and Federal estate taxes are deductible under section 2053(a)(2) only as they accrue and become certain because with fluctuating interest rates it is impossible to make a reasonable estimate of the amount of interest involved and prepayment of the taxes would eliminate the interest. 81 T.C. at 251.

Petitioner concedes that Bailly is on point, but argues that the reasons we gave for not allowing the deduction could be overcome by requiring respondent to enter into either a closing agreement or a compromise agreement under which the estate would be allowed the deduction in return for agreeing to pay any increased estate tax resulting from failure to make the interest payments. However, this Court does not have authority to require respondent to enter into such a closing or compromise agreement.

Post-Death Interest on Debt Incurred by Decedent. On December 19, 1979, the decedent through a power of attorney, executed a promissory note payable on December 19, 1980 in the amount of $1.5 million dollars to Texas Commerce Bank. The estate paid the note at maturity, without renewing or extending it. The payment included interest in the amount of $118,134.67, which had accrued subsequent to the decedent's death.

Post-death interest paid on a debt incurred by a decedent during his life and not renewed by his estate is deductible under section 2053(a)(2) if the following conditions are met: (1) the interest expense is actually and necessarily incurred in the administration of the decedent's estate; and (2) the expense is allowable as an administration expense under local law. Estate of Wheless v. Commissioner, 72 T.C. 470, 479-480 (1979); Estate of Webster v. Commissioner, 65 T.C. 968, 981 (1976).

With respect to the first condition, it is stipulated that the interest expense was actually incurred by petitioner, and under our reasoning in Estate of Webster, we find that the interest was necessarily incurred because the retirement of the $1.5 million debt prior to its maturity would have required the liquidation of estate assets under unfavorable conditions.

We addressed the second condition in Estate of

Wheless, where we noted that chapter 7, section 242 of the Texas Probate Code (Vernon 1956), provides that:

Personal representatives of estates shall also be entitled to all necessary and reasonable expenses incurred by them in the preservation, safe-keeping, and management of the estate and in collecting or attempting to collect claims or debts, and in recovering or attempting to recover property to which the estate has a title or claim, and all reasonable attorney's fees, necessarily incurred in connection with the proceedings and management of such estate, on satisfactory proof to the court.

72 T.C. at 480. Relying on this statute, as well as Estate of Todd v. Commissioner, 57 T.C. 288 (1971) and King v. Battaglia, 38 Tex. Civ. App. 28, 84 S.W. 839 (1905), we concluded that interest is allowable as an administration expense under Texas law. 72 T.C. at 480. We also found that such expense was "necessary and reasonably incurred by [the executors] in the preservation, safe-keeping, and management of the estate." 72 T.C. at 480. We believe that this conclusion is equally applicable to the present case. Consequently, we conclude that the interest expense is allowable as an administration expense under Texas law and is deductible by the estate under section 2053(a)(2).

Decision will be entered under Rule 155.

Notes

1. All section references are to the Internal Revenue Code of 1954, as amended, unless otherwise indicated. All rule references are to the Tax Court Rules of Practice and Procedure unless otherwise provided.

2. Dan's acts with respect to the creation of the partnership and the contribution of decedent's assets thereto under the power of attorney were reviewed in detail and approved by the District Court of Fort Bend County, Texas in September 1979 in an adversarial proceeding brought by decedent's next friend who alleged, and the court found, that on August 12, 1979, decedent had suffered a stroke and had fall-

en and broken both shoulders. The Court further found that the partnership constituted "a means for the proper and necessary management of the properties of [decedent]" and that the partnership agreement was "advantageous to and in the best interests of [decedent]."

3. In other words, decedent's right, as a general partner, to dissolve and liquidate the partnership increased the value of the limited partnership interest by the difference of $26,555,020.

Glossary

CLAT — A charitable lead annuity trust. The CLAT pays a preset, fixed income interest to a charity for a term of years or the lifetime of a person or persons. At the end of the specified term the assets go to a non-charitable beneficiary, usually the donor's children. It is a taxable trust.

CLUT — A charitable lead unitrust. It is identical to the CLAT *except* for the fact that the payments to the charity will vary each year as the value of the trust changes. It is not used as frequently as the CLAT.

CRAT — A charitable remainder annuity trust. The CRAT is similar to the CRUT, except that the income recipients receive an income that is fixed, regardless of the performance of the trust's assets. It is also a tax-*exempt* trust.

CRUT — A charitable remainder unitrust. The CRUT pays an income interest to *non*-charitable recipients, usually the donor(s), for lifetime or a number of years not to exceed twenty. The income is a variable amount each year, as it is a percentage of the trust's changing assets. At the end of that term, the trust corpus must go to a qualified charity. It is a tax-*exempt* trust.

FLP — Family limited partnership. A limited partnership under state law, usually drafted in such a way that it causes the limited partnership units to "lose value" for transfer tax purposes.

Grantor — The grantor is generally the person who establishes and transfers corpus to a trust.

Grantor Trust — This refers to a trust that will be taxed to the grantor for income tax purposes. There are reasons why a grantor may want to have a trust treated as a grantor trust for income tax purposes, while not being a grantor trust for estate tax purposes.

GRAT — A grantor retained annuity trust. It is a split-interest trust from which the grantor (usually the parents) receive an income that is fixed at the outset of the trust. At the end of the trust term the trust corpus goes to non-charitable beneficiaries, usually the children. It is used to move assets to the next generation at a discount.

GST — Generation-skipping trust. It is used to control assets for skip generations (grandchildren on down), and is meant to qualify for the $1 million GSTT exemption.

GSTT — Generation skipping transfer tax. It is a 55 percent surtax imposed on transfers to a skip person. A skip person is two or more generations younger than the transferor. There is a $1 million exemption per transferor available before the tax is imposed. The GSTT is in addition to any gift or estate tax.

IGT — Intentional grantor trust. This is a trust that will be out of the grantor's estate for estate tax purposes, but is considered the grantor's property for income tax purposes. It is often called a "defective" grantor trust, as the attorney drafting the document must create a defect in the trust that causes it to be a grantor trust.

ILIT — An irrevocable life insurance trust. This trust is used to hold life insurance and other assets to keep the insurance out of the estates of the parents, while protecting the assets from creditors of the heirs, etc.

Income Recipient — The individual or entity receiving the income payments from a split interest trust. Also referred to as income "beneficiaries."

NIMCRUT — A net income with makeup CRUT, it pays only that which is defined as "net-income from year to year. However, if the income is less than the stated payout rate, a contingent "IOU" is booked that can only be paid out of excess income in a future year.

QPRT — A qualified personal residence trust. Like the GRAT, this trust is used to get assets to children at a discount. Its distinctive feature is that the only eligible asset is a personal residence of the grantor, which the grantor continues to use for the term of the trust.

Remainderman — The individual or entity that receives the assets remaining in a split interest trust at the end of the trust term.

Endnotes

Chapter 1

1. IRC § 2001(a) states "A tax is hereby imposed on the transfer of the taxable estate of every decedent who is a citizen or resident of the United States." The concept of a transfer tax versus a property tax or inheritance tax is very important in wealth transfer planning because the tax is on the value of that transferred. This is the "first fundamental" in the outline of presentations done by S. Stacy Eastland, Esq. (Baker & Botts in Houston, Texas) entitled *The Art of Making Uncle Sam Your Assignee Instead of Your Senior Partner: The Use of Family Limited Partnerships in Estate Planning*. Many of the creative techniques of advanced estate planning are dependent on the importance of the estate and gift taxes being treated as a tax on the transfer of property, and not a tax on the property itself.

    Reg. § 20.2033-1(a) further clarifies this point in stating "Various statutory provisions which exempt bonds, notes, bills, and certificates of indebtedness of the Federal Government or its agencies and the interest thereon from taxation are generally not applicable to the estate tax, since such tax is an excise tax on the transfer of property at death and is not a tax on the property transferred."

2. People generally talk about the "$600,000 *exemption*," but this terminology is not accurate. Before the Economic Recovery Tax Act (ERTA) in 1981, there was an exemption that reduced the taxable estate before starting taxation in a low tax bracket. Now the tax-

able estate is calculated without any "exemption, "to arrive at the taxable estate. Then a $192,800 credit is applied which offsets the tax due in the first $600,000. The difference is more than semantic because of the steeply graduated scale of the tax.

3. There is an excellent, brief discussion of trust law principles and a trustee's duties in *Charitable Gift Planning News*, Vol. 14/No. 2, February, 1996 pgs. 4ff. The trustee has a primary duty to the trust beneficiaries and can be subject to liability if he does not properly manage the trust assets and impartially carry out trust terms.

4. The term "grantor" is used in discussing grantor trusts. A trust can be a grantor trust for income tax purposes (see IRC § 674-677) without the trust being included in the grantor's taxable estate. See Coleman, Virginia *The Grantor Trust: Yesterday's Disaster, Today's Delight, Tomorrow's? University of Miami School of Law Institute on Estate Planning* (1996)

5. Generation-skipping was severely limited when IRC § 2611 was added by the Tax Reform Act of 1986. It describes "taxable distributions," "taxable terminations," and "direct skips." If generation skips are made that exceed the $1 million exemption an additional flat tax of 55 percent is imposed on the transfer. This topic is extremely complicated and should always be discussed with a professional who has a great deal of experience drafting GSTs. It was only December, 1995 when the Treasury released final regulations clarifying the GST provisions of the Internal Revenue Code.

6. A few states have no rule against perpetuities so the trust can continue for several generations. There is a good discussion of this as to North Dakota trusts in *Trusts & Estates*.

7. See IRC § 2036(a)

8. There are three possible taxes imposed on the transfer of IRA or qualified plan balances on death. The net distribution is taxed as a part of the overall estate, just like any other asset. If the distribution goes to grandchildren or a non-exempt GST, the 55 percent generation-skipping transfer tax is applied. Finally, when the family receives income, it is taxed at ordinary income rates as income in respect of a decedent (see IRC § 691).

Chapter 2

1. There is a good discussion on point in Waxenberg, Henry, *Comparing the Advantages of Estates and Revocable Trusts..*, Vol. 22, *Estate Planning*, 09-01-1995, pp 265. For another view see Hance, Barbara, *Proceed Cautiously When Considering a Living Trust..*, Vol. 35, *Westchester County Business Journal*, 06-10-1996, pp 21.

2. Most practitioners draft the trust so the credit shelter trust will receive the maximum amount that it can, while still having no net federal estate tax. Then, as the amount of the credit is increased but the trust is not amended, nothing is lost. However, with the myriad of changes included in TRA '97, it would be prudent to review all wills and trusts.

3. For a good article that discusses the major issues involved see Cavanaugh, Robert, *Tax court rebuffs IRS view that power to remove trustee is retained control..*, Vol. 80, *Journal of Taxation*, 03-01-1994, pp 144. The concept of an ascertainable standard is found in the code.. General powers of appointment cause trust assets over which a decedent has such a power to be includable in the gross estate. In IRC § 2041 (b)(1)(A) an exception is found as follows:

(1) GENERAL POWER OF APPOINTMENT

The term "general power of appointment" means a power which is exercisable in favor of the decedent, his estate, his creditors, or the creditors of his estate; except that —

(A) A power to consume, invade, or appropriate property for the benefit of the decedent which is limited by *an ascertainable standard* relating to the health, education, support, or maintenance of the decedent shall not be deemed a general power of appointment

Reg 20.2041-1(c)(2) provides:

(2) POWERS LIMITED BY AN ASCERTAINABLE STANDARD.

A power to consume, invade, or appropriate income or corpus, or both, for the benefit of the decedent which is limited by an ascertainable standard relating to the health, education, support, or maintenance of the decedent is, by reason of section 2041(b)(1)(A), not a general power of appointment. A power is limited by such a standard if the extent of the holder's duty to exercise and not to exercise the power is reasonably measurable in terms of his needs for health, education, or support (or any combination of them). As used in this subparagraph, the words "support" and "maintenance" are synonymous and their meaning is not limited to the bare necessities of life. A power to use property for the comfort, welfare, or happiness of the holder of the power is not limited by the requisite standard. Examples of powers which are limited by the requisite standard are powers exercisable for the holder's "support," "support in reasonable comfort," "maintenance in health and reasonable comfort," "support in his accustomed manner of living," "education, including college and professional education,"health," and "medical, dental, hospital and nursing expenses and expenses of invalidism." In determining whether a power is limited by an ascertainable standard, it is immaterial whether the beneficiary is required to exhaust his other income before the power can be exercised."

There is a whole body of judicial interpretation of what congress meant by "ascertainable standard," and bypass trusts that contained overly broad powers were thrown back in the estate of the surviving spouse. See, e.g., Estate of Sowell v. Commissioner, 708 F.2d 1564, 1568 (10th Cir. 1983) (invasion of trust corpus in case of emergency or illness is an ascertainable standard under section 2041(b)(1)(A)); Gaskill v. United States, 561 F. Supp. 73, 78 (D. Kan. 1983) (life estate with power of disposition but not to consume the proceeds did not create general power of appointment under section 2041(b)(1)(A)), aff'd mem., 787 F.2d 1446 (10th Cir. 1986)

4. A marital deduction is allowable for QTIP property under IRC § 2056 (b)(7). It states:

(7) ELECTION WITH RESPECT TO LIFE ESTATE FOR SURVIVING SPOUSE

(A) IN GENERAL

In the case of qualified terminable interest property —

(i)   for purposes of subsection (a), such property shall be treated as passing to the surviving spouse, and

(ii) for purposes of paragraph (1)(A), no part of such property shall be treated as passing to any person other than the surviving spouse.

(B) QUALIFIED TERMINABLE INTEREST PROPERTY DEFINED

For purposes of this paragraph —

(i)   IN GENERAL

The term "qualified terminable interest property" means property —

(I)   which passes from the decedent,

(II) in which the surviving spouse has a qualifying income interest for life, and

(III) to which an election under this paragraph applies.

The qualifying income interest under IRC § 2056(b)(7)(B)(ii) is defined as

(ii) QUALIFYING INCOME INTEREST FOR LIFE

The surviving spouse has a qualifying income interest for life if —

(I)   the surviving spouse is entitled to all the income from the property, payable annually or at more frequent intervals, or has a usufruct interest for life in the property, and

(II) no person has a power to appoint any part of the property to any person other than the surviving spouse.

The major purpose in establishing a QTIP trust is control. The deceased spouse could get the same marital deduction by outright bequest to the surviving spouse or to a marital trust containing a general power of appointment. The QTIP will generally have restrictions on access to principal and only a limited power of appointment that precludes the survivor from leaving corpus to a subsequent spouse or other individual not acceptable to the decedent creator of the QTIP.

Chapter 3

1. All split interest trusts and related gifts are valued under IRC §7520.
SECTION 7520. VALUATION TABLES

(a) GENERAL RULE

For purposes of this title, the value of any annuity, any interest for life or a term of years, or any remainder or reversionary interest shall be determined —

> (1) under tables prescribed by the Secretary, and
>
> (2) by using an interest rate (rounded to the nearest 2/10ths of 1 percent) equal to 120 percent of the Federal midterm rate in effect under section 1274(d)(1) for the month in which the valuation date falls.

If an income, estate, or gift tax charitable contribution is allowable for any part of the property transferred, the taxpayer may elect to use such Federal midterm rate for either of the 2 months preceding the month in which the valuation date falls for purposes of paragraph (2). In the case of transfers of more than 1 interest in the same property with respect to which the taxpayer may use the same rate under paragraph (2), the taxpayer shall use the same rate with respect to each such interest.

(b) SECTION NOT TO APPLY FOR CERTAIN PURPOSES

This section shall not apply for purposes of part I of subchapter D of chapter 1 or any other provision specified in regulations.

(c) TABLES

> (1) IN GENERAL
>
> The tables prescribed by the Secretary for purposes of subsection (a) shall contain valuation factors for a series of interest rate categories.
>
> (2) INITIAL TABLE
>
> Not later than the day 3 months after the date of the enactment of this section, the Secretary shall prescribe initial tables for purposes of subsection (a). Such tables may be based on the same mortality experience as used for purposes of section 2031 on the date of the enactment of this section.
>
> (3) REVISION FOR RECENT MORTALITY CHARGES
>
> Not later than December 31, 1989, the Secretary shall revise the initial tables prescribed for purposes of subsection (a) to take into account the most recent mortality experience available as of the time of such revision. Such tables shall be revised not less frequently than once each 10 years thereafter to take into account the most recent mortality experience available as of the time of the revision.

2. In a very readable article Andrew Painer, a CPA with Ernst & Young writes a concise explanation of various split interest trusts. He says, "This column is written with an eye towards the sales floor where split-interest transactions are presented to high net worth clients. It is hoped that the following discussion will benefit the new age of financial planners and clients by charting a flight plan miles above the technical detail where needs can be identified and satisfied by pulling the right arrow from the quiver of split-interest transactions." Painter, Andrew, *A simplified marketing approach for split-interest trusts..*, Vol. 23, *Estate Planning*, 06-01-1996, pp 227.

3. In 1988 congress formalized the calculation of the interests in a split interest trust. The interest rates to be used in the calculation are determined under IRC§7520:

SECTION 7520. VALUATION TABLES

(a) GENERAL RULE

For purposes of this title, the value of any annuity, any interest for life or a term of years, or any remainder or reversionary interest shall be determined —

(1) under tables prescribed by the Secretary, and

(2) by using an interest rate (rounded to the nearest 2/10ths of 1 percent) equal to 120 percent of the Federal midterm rate in effect under section 1274(d)(1) for the month in which the valuation date falls.

If an income, estate, or gift tax charitable contribution is allowable for any part of the property transferred, the taxpayer may elect to use such Federal midterm rate for either of the 2 months preceding the month in which the valuation date falls for purposes of paragraph (2). In the case of transfers of more than 1 interest in the same property with respect to which the taxpayer may use the same rate under paragraph (2), the taxpayer shall use the same rate with respect to each such interest.

An example of the tables prescribed by the Secretary (as used for charitable remainder trusts can be found in Reg 1.884-4:

TABLE D SHOWING THE PRESENT WORTH OF A REMAINDER INTEREST POSTPONED FOR A TERM CERTAIN IN A CHARITABLE REMAINDER UNITRUST APPLICABLE AFTER APRIL 30, 1989

ADJUSTED PAYOUT RATE

YEARS	4.2 %	4.4 %	4.6 %	4.8 %	5.0 %	5.2 %
1	.958000	.956000	.954000	.952000	.950000	.948000
2	.917764	.913936	.910116	.906304	.902500	.898704
3	.879218	.873723	.868251	.862801	.857375	.851971
4	.842291	.835279	.828311	.821387	.814506	.807669
5	.806915	.798527	.790209	.781960	.773781	.765670
6	.773024	.763392	.753859	.744426	.735092	.725855
7	.740557	.729802	.719182	.708694	.698337	.688111
8	.709454	.697691	.686099	.674677	.663420	.652329
9	.679657	.666993	.654539	.642292	.630249	.618408
10	.651111	.637645	.624430	.611462	.598737	.586251
11	.623764	.609589	.595706	.582112	.568800	.555766
12	.597566	.582767	.568304	.554170	.540360	.526866
13	.572469	.557125	.542162	.527570	.513342	.499469
14	.548425	.532611	.517222	.502247	.487675	.473496
15	.525391	.509177	.493430	.478139	.463291	.448875
16	.503325	.486773	.470732	.455188	.440127	.425533
17	.482185	.465355	.449079	.433339	.418120	.403405

18	.461933	.444879	.428421	.412539	.397214	.382428
19	.442532	.425304	.408714	.392737	.377354	.362542
20	.423946	.406591	.389913	.373886	.358486	.343690

Similar tables are used for various income and remainder interests in the various types of split interest trusts including GRATs, QPRTs, etc.

Chapter 4

1. IRC §664(d) defines the two as follows:
    (1) CHARITABLE REMAINDER ANNUITY TRUST
       For purposes of this section, a charitable remainder annuity trust is a trust —
       (A) from which a sum certain (which is not less than 5 percent of the initial net fair market value of all property placed in trust) is to be paid, not less often than annually, to one or more persons (at least one of which is not an organization described in section 170(c) and, in the case of individuals, only to an individual who is living at the time of the creation of the trust) for a term of years (not in excess of 20 years) or for the life or lives of such individual or individuals,
       (B) from which no amount other than the payments described in subparagraph (A) may be paid to or for the use of any person other than an organization described in section 170(c), and
       (C) following the termination of the payments described in subparagraph (A), the remainder interest in the trust is to be transferred to, or for the use of, an organization described in section 170(c) or is to be retained by the trust for such a use.
    (2) CHARITABLE REMAINDER UNITRUST
       For purposes of this section, a charitable remainder unitrust is a trust —
       (A) from which a fixed percentage (which is not less than 5 percent) of the net fair market value of its assets, valued annually, is to be paid, not less often than annually, to one or more persons (at least one of which is not an organization described in section 170(c) and, in the case of individuals, only to an individual who is living at the time of the creation of the trust) for a term of years (not in excess of 20 years) or for the life or lives of such individual or individuals,
       (B) from which no amount other than the payments described in subparagraph (A) may be paid to or for the use of any person other than an organization described in section 170(c), and
       (C) following the termination of the payments described in subparagraph (A), the remainder interest in the trust is to be transferred to, or for the use of, an organization described in section 170(c) or is to be retained by the trust for such a use.
2. A CRT is a tax-exempt trust, but there is a major land mine that could

blow up in the face of the unwary advisor or trustee. A CRT loses its exempt status for any year in which the trust has Unrelated Business Taxable Income (UBTI). If this occurs in the initial year of the trust when appreciated assets are usually sold, the entire gain would be taxable to the trust. UBTI comes primarily from two sources, an operating business, or debt-financed income. For example, if a donor transferred a motel to a CRT, and the motel continued to operate in the trust until sold, the profits from the motel would be "business" profits that are unrelated to the exempt purpose of the trust. If the net profits were $5,000 for the year, and during the same year the motel were sold with a $1 million gain, the trust would be considered a taxable trust for the year and the gain would be taxable. Margin accounts can create UBTI problems, as can owning REIT shares. If anything other than stocks, bonds, cash or non-operating real property are contributed to or owned by a CRT, expert counsel must be sought.

3. While the CRT itself is an exempt entity and pays no income taxes under normal circumstances, a donor can actually pay capital gains taxes over time by selecting a payout rate higher than the assumed rate of return on the investments made by the trust. Under the four-tier accounting system used for split-interest charitable trusts, the payment to the income beneficiaries of amount in excess of current earning will be treated as long-term capital gains to the extenst such gains were earned by the trust upon the sale of the contributed assets. See Appendix A for a more detailed discussion of four tier accounting.

4. There is a *de facto* conflict between donors and the charitable remaindermen due to the very nature of split interest trusts. The higher the payout rate, the less that will be left for charity. A financial advisor can easily evaluate the benefits of various payout rates by discounting cash flows to present value. But even that does not address the real issues. For the most part a charitable remainder trust that is planned *for the donor* will address the income needs of the income beneficiaries (usually the donors). With younger income beneficiaries a lower payout rate will generally be in order, resulting in payments that keep up with inflation over time. This usually benefits both the charity and the donor, as the income rises over long periods of time and the institution receives a larger endowment.

However, with older donors this may not be the case. If the donors need a higher level of *current* income, it is better to have a higher payout, even if the corpus is somewhat depleted over time. Nonprofits do not like the higher payout trusts (especially when they are the trustees), but if properly planned and presented, it should never be a problem. If the donors cannot have enough income from a 5 to 7 percent CRT, but would with a 10 to 12 percent trust, it should be recommended. Granted it decreases the charitable remainder, but the remainder would be even less if the donor sold the assets in question, paid taxes, spent the cash flow as needed, and made a bequest of those assets at death. Nonprofits are generally delighted to receive bequests. There is no difference between a $500,000 bequest and a remainder interest in a $1,000,000 12 percent CRT, that due to its high payout rate shrinks to $500,000 at the donors' death.

5. In most instances the charitable income tax deduction is calculated by taking the fair market value of the assets and multiplying that value by the difference between the whole and the value of the retained income interest. The resulting deduction is then further restricted by the character of the asset and the donor's adjusted gross income (AGI). Where the contributed assets are appreciated capital assets and the charity is a public charity described in IRC§ 170(b)(1)(A), the deduction allowable in one year is limited to 30 percent of AGI:

(C) SPECIAL LIMITATION WITH RESPECT TO CONTRIBUTIONS DESCRIBED IN SUBPARAGRAPH (A) OF CERTAIN CAPITAL GAIN PROPERTY

(i) In the case of charitable contributions described in subparagraph (A) of capital gain property to which subsection (e)(1)(B) does not apply, the total amount of contributions of such property which may be taken into account under subsection (a) for any taxable year shall not exceed 30 percent of the taxpayer's contribution base for such year. For purposes of this subsection, contributions of capital gain property to which this subparagraph applies shall be taken into account after all other charitable contributions (other than charitable contributions to which subparagraph (D) applies).

(ii) If charitable contributions described in subparagraph (A) of capital gain property to which clause (i) applies exceeds 30 percent of the taxpayer's contribution base for any taxable year, such excess shall be treated, in a manner consistent with the rules of subsection (d)(1), as a charitable contribution of capital gain property to which clause (i) applies in each of the 5 succeeding taxable years in order of time.

(iii) At the election of the taxpayer (made at such time and in such manner as the Secretary prescribes by regulations), subsection (e)(1) shall apply to all contributions of capital gain property (to which subsection (e)(1)(B) does not otherwise apply) made by the taxpayer during the taxable year. If such an election is made, clauses (i) and (ii) shall not apply to contributions of capital gain property made during the taxable year, and, in applying subsection (d)(1) for such taxable year with respect to contributions of capital gain property made in any prior contribution year for which an election was not made under this clause, such contributions shall be reduced as if subsection (e)(1) had applied to such contributions in the year in which made.

(iv) For purposes of this paragraph, the term "capital gain property" means with respect to any contribution, any capital asset the sale of which at its fair market value at the time of the contribution would have resulted in gain which would have been long-term capital gain. For purposes of the preceding sentence, any property which is property used in the trade or business (as defined in section 1231(b)) shall be treated as a capital asset. IRC§ 170(b)(1)(C)

If the charitable remaindermen are not public charities described in IRC§ 170(b)(1)(A), the annual limitations are greater:

(D) SPECIAL LIMITATION WITH RESPECT TO CONTRIBUTIONS OF CAPITAL GAIN PROPERTY TO ORGANIZATIONS NOT DESCRIBED IN SUBPARAGRAPH (A)

(i) IN GENERAL

In the case of charitable contributions (other than charitable contributions to which subparagraph (A) applies) of capital gain property, the total amount of such contributions of such property taken into account under subsection (a) for any taxable year shall not exceed the lesser of —

(I) 20 percent of the taxpayer's contribution base for the taxable year, or

(II) the excess of 30 percent of the taxpayer's contribution base for the taxable year over the amount of the contributions of capital gain property to which subparagraph (C) applies.

For purposes of this subsection, contributions of capital gain property to which this subparagraph applies shall be taken into account after all other charitable contributions.

6. This problem has led to significant pressure on the IRS to allow for trusts to start as net income trusts and then "flip" to standard trusts after the illiquid assets are sold. Such "flip trusts" are not provided for in the statute, but Proposed Regulations were issued in April, 1997 that will permit such a design where illiquid assets constitute more than 90 percent of a CRT's assets. Many professionals who commented to the IRS regarding the proposed regulations suggested a lower threshold. The final regulations, likely to be issued in 1998 or 1999 will determine the percentage applicable.

7. Sometimes referred to as a "Type 2" CRT, it generally provides the maximum to charity and the minimum cash flow to the income beneficiaries. It could be ideal for people who want only the limited amount available from dividends, and who want to see that principal is never invaded. Even though the charity is likely to end up with more money, the tax deduction does not increase just because a net income trust is being used.

8. The concept of income in a charitable trust is not the same as in tax or general accounting. In discussing net income from a NIMCRUT

you must be aware of fiduciary accounting principles. Most states have a principal and income act that details what is attributed to corpus, and what is considered income. In several states there is great latitude left to the trustee or the drafter of the trust. For example, in California the trust document can define gains realized on the sale of capital assets (capital gain for tax purposes) as income for trust purposes. This difference becomes very important in times of low interest rates and where donors want to have a somewhat flexible, higher payment flow. Many practitioners question this flexibility, but the IRS has issued letter rulings directly on point. A very interesting ruling, PLR94442017 (7/19/94), showing the flexibility possible follows:

PLR94442017

This responds to a letter from your authorized representative dated November 10, 1993, as supplemented March 9 and May 24, 1994, in which he asks us on your behalf to rule on the qualification of Trust as a charitable remainder unitrust under section 664 of the Internal Revenue Code.

According to section 4.01(39) of Rev. Proc. 94-3, 1994-1 I.R.B. 79, the Service ordinarily will not rule on whether a charitable remainder trust that provides for annuity or unitrust payments for one or two measuring lives satisfies the requirements described in section 664 of the Code. In addition, according to sections 4.01(16), (44), and (46) of Rev. Proc. 94-3, the Service ordinarily will not rule on whether a transfer to a charitable remainder trust described in section 664 that provides for annuity or unitrust payments for one or two measuring lives qualifies for charitable deductions under sections 170(f)(2)(A), 2055(e)(2)(A), and 2522(c)(2)(A).

In lieu of seeking the Service's advance approval of a charitable remainder unitrust, taxpayers are directed to follow the sample provisions for charitable remainder unitrusts outlined in Rev. Proc. 90-31, 1990-1 C.B. 539 The Service will recognize as meeting all of the requirements of a charitable remainder unitrust any trust substantially following one of the sample forms of trust in Rev Proc 90-31, provided that the trust operates in a manner consistent with the terms of the instrument creating the trust and provided it is a valid trust under applicable local law For transfers to a qualifying charitable remainder unitrust, the present value of the remainder interest will be deductible under sections 170(f)(2)(A), 2055(e)(2)(A), and 2522(c)(2)(A) if the charitable beneficiary otherwise meets all of the requirements of these sections. Taxpayers, however, have submitted a trust agreement with substantive provisions not included in, or different from, the sample provisions outlined in Rev. Proc. 90-31 or Rev. Rul 72-395, 1972-2 C.B. 340, as modified by Rev. Rul. 80-123, 1980-1 C.B. 205, and Rev. Rul. 82-128, 1982-2 C.B. 71, and clarified by Rev. Rul. 82-165, 1982-2 C.B. 117 Therefore, we will rule on whether these substantive modifications disqualify Trust as a charitable remainder unitrust under section 664 of the Code, if it is otherwise qualified.

FACTS

Taxpayers are husband and wife. They will establish Trust, to be governed by the trust agreement and the laws of State. Trust is intended to qualify as a charitable remainder unitrust for federal tax purposes.

Taxpayer A will contribute approximately a shares of Company to Trust. Taxpayers may make additional contributions to Trust.

Charity, an organization exempt from tax under section 170(c) of the Code, will act as trustee of Trust. However, Taxpayers retain the right to remove Charity as trustee, without cause, and to appoint as successor trustee any individual or entity, including themselves.

The unitrust amount to be paid to Taxpayers is limited to Trust's net income. If Trust's net income exceeds 7 percent of Trust's net fair market value, the trustee will apply the excess to any deficiencies in prior year unitrust payments resulting from the net income limitation.

The trustee will pay the unitrust amount to Taxpayers in equal shares for their joint lives, and then to the survivor for the survivor's life Trust will terminate at the survivor's death, and the trustee will pay the charitable remainder to organizations described in sections 170(c), 2055(a), and 2522(a) of the Code.

Taxpayer A, as investment manager, retains the right to direct the investment of all trust assets, except for those having no readily ascertainable market value. Taxpayer A expects to invest some of the assets of Trust in Partnership.

Taxpayer A is a general partner of Partnership. He also is a managing director and employee of Firm, a registered investment advisor that provides all investment advice and management to Partnership. Partnership invests funds received from its partners. Partnership pays Firm a quarterly fee of .25 percent of the market value of Partnership and reimburses Firm for certain expenses up to .50 percent of the year-end market value of Partnership. Taxpayer A is compensated by Firm for his work in connection with the investment advice and management services Firm provides Partnership. Partnership interests are valued quarterly and may be withdrawn quarterly after 30 days notice.

In addition to ruling that the provisions of the trust agreement not contained in Rev. Proc. 90-31 or Rev. Rul. 72-395, as modified and clarified, will not disqualify Trust as a charitable remainder unitrust (Ruling Request 1), Taxpayers have asked us to rule that the investment of trust assets in Partnership at the direction of Taxpayer A or B acting as the investment manager of Trust will not disqualify Trust as a charitable remainder unitrust (Ruling Request 2).

LAW & ANALYSIS

RULING REQUEST 1

Paragraph 13 of the trust agreement allows Taxpayers to terminate the appointment of the trustee and to appoint a successor trustee, which may be one or both of Taxpayers.

Section 1.664-1(a)(4) of the Income Tax Regulations provides that, in order for a trust to be a charitable remainder trust, it must meet the definition of and function exclusively as a charitable remainder trust from the creation of the trust Solely for purposes of section 664 and the regulations thereunder, the trust will be deemed to be created at the earliest time that neither the grantor nor any other person is treated as the owner of the entire trust under subpart E, part 1, subchapter J, chapter 1, subtitle A of the Code (relating to grantors and others treated as substantial owners), but in no event prior to the time property is first transferred to the trust. For purposes of the preceding sentence, neither the grantor nor his spouse shall be treated as the owner of the trust under such subpart E merely because the grantor or his spouse is named as a recipient.

Section 1.664-3(a)(3)(ii) of the regulations provides that a trust is not a charitable remainder unitrust if any person has the power to alter the amount to be paid to any named person other than an organization described in section 170(c) of the Code if such power would cause any person to be treated as the owner of the trust, or any portion thereof, if subpart E, part 1, subchapter J, chapter 1, subtitle A were applicable to such trust.

Section 674(a) of the Code provides that the grantor shall be treated as the owner of any portion of a trust in respect of which the beneficial enjoyment of the corpus or income therefrom is subject to a power of disposition exercisable by the grantor or a non adverse party, or both, without the approval or consent of any adverse party.

Rev. Rul. 77-285, 1977-2 C.B. 213, holds that an otherwise qualifying charitable remainder trust that authorizes the grantor to remove the trustee for any reason and substitute any person, including himself, is not disqualified under section 664 of the Code as long as the trustee has no discretion to allocate the specified distribution between beneficiaries.

The trust agreement provides for the distribution to Taxpayers of a fixed unitrust amount. The trustee has no discretion to allocate this amount between Taxpayers. This provision complies with section 1.664-3(a)(3)(ii) of the regulations. Therefore, the authority of Taxpayers under paragraph 13 of the trust agreement to terminate the appointment of the trustee and to appoint a successor trustee, including one or both of themselves, does not disqualify Trust as a charitable remainder unitrust, if it is otherwise qualified.

Paragraph 14 of the trust agreement appoints first Taxpayer A, then Taxpayer B, as the investment manager of Trust and gives the investment manager authority to direct the investment of trust assets (other than assets having no readily ascertainable market value).

Section 675(4) of the Code provides that the grantor shall be treated as the owner of any portion of a trust in respect of which a power of administration is exercisable in a nonfiduciary capacity by any person without the approval or consent of any person in a fiduciary capacity For purposes of this paragraph, the term "power of administration" includes a power to control the investment of the trust funds either by directing investments or reinvestments, or by vetoing proposed investments or reinvestments, to the extent that the trust funds consist of stocks or securities of corporations in which the holdings of the grantor and the trust are significant from the viewpoint of voting control.

Section 1.675-1(b)(4) of the regulations provides that, if a power is exercisable by a person as trustee, it is presumed that the power is exercisable in a fiduciary capacity primarily in the interests of the beneficiaries. This presumption may be rebutted only by clear and convincing proof that the power is not exercisable primarily in the interests of the beneficiaries. If a power is not exercisable by a person as trustee, the determination of whether the power is exercisable in a fiduciary or a nonfiduciary capacity depends on all the terms of the trust and the circumstances surrounding its creation and administration.

The trust agreement provides that Taxpayer A for life, then Taxpayer B for life, shall serve as the investment manager of Trust, with the authority to designate others to direct trust investments or to direct the trustee to make certain investments. The investment manager may direct the investment of trust assets in specific partnerships, pooled funds, common trust funds, or mutual funds which may be managed by the investment manager. The investment manager may direct the investment of trust assets in specified publicly traded stocks and bonds. The only limit to this investment authority, other than the stipulation that it be exercised in a fiduciary capacity, is the provision in paragraph 15 of the trust agreement for an independent investment manager to determine the value and direct the investment of trust assets having no readily ascertainable fair market value. These investment provisions are very broad and could involve the investment of trust funds in stocks or securities of corporations in which the holdings of the grantor and the trust are significant from the viewpoint of voting control. Therefore, only the circumstances surrounding the administration of Trust will determine whether the investment manager holds a power of administration within the meaning of section 675(4) of the Code or whether such a power is held in a fiduciary capacity. This is a question of fact, the determination of which must be deferred until the federal income tax returns of the parties involved have been examined by the office of the appropriate District Director. Therefore, we can not determine at this time whether the authority of the investment manager under paragraph 14 of the trust agreement to direct the investment of trust assets disqualifies Trust as a charitable remainder unitrust.

Paragraph 15 of the trust agreement provides for the appointment of an independent investment manager meeting the qualifications of an "independent" trustee under section 674(c) of the Code, to value and direct the investment of assets having no readily ascertainable market value.

The legislative history of section 664 of the Code (Tax Reform Act 1969) indicates that Congress — contemplated that a charitable contribution deduction would be denied where assets which do not have an objective, ascertainable market value, such as real estate or stock in a closely held corporation, are transferred in trust, unless an independent trustee is the sole party responsible for making the annual determination of value.

H.R. Rep. No. 413 (Part 1), 91st Cong., 1st Sess. 60 (1969); reprinted 1969-3 C.B. 200, 239.

The trust agreement provides for the appointment of an independent investment manager whenever Trust holds any asset not having a readily ascertainable fair market value, such as the stock of a closely held corporation The independent investment manager has sole authority to value these assets and to determine whether, and under what terms, to dispose of these assets. The independent investment manager is required to be an "independent trustee", as that term is used in section 674(c) of the Code. These provisions do not conflict with any of the regulations under section 664 (the requirement for an independent trustee to value trust assets having no readily ascertainable market value is not specifically incorporated in the section 664 regulations). However, the provisions are very broad and could involve the investment of trust funds in stocks or securities of corporations in which the holdings of the grantor and the trust are significant from the viewpoint of voting control. Therefore, only the circumstances surrounding the administration of Trust will determine whether the independent investment manager holds a power of administration within the meaning of section 675(4) of the Code or whether such a power is held in a fiduciary capacity. This is a question of fact, the determination of which must be deferred until the federal income tax returns of the parties involved have been examined by the office of the appropriate District Director. Therefore, we can not determine at this time whether the authority of the independent investment manager under paragraph 15 of the trust agreement to direct the investment of trust assets having no readily ascertainable market value disqualifies Trust as a charitable remainder unitrust.

Paragraphs 8 and 21 of the trust agreement permit the trustee to distribute Trust assets to charitable organizations during the lines of Taxpayers only with the consent of Taxpayers or the survivor.

Under section 1.664-3(a)(4) of the regulations, the governing instrument of a charitable remainder unitrust may provide that any amount other than the unitrust amount may be paid in the discretion of the trustee to an organization described in section 170(c) of the Code provided that, in the case of distributions in kind, the adjusted basis of the property distributed is fairly representative of the adjusted basis of the property available for payment on the date of payment.

The trust agreement provides for the distribution of trust assets at any time to qualified charitable organizations. If trust assets are distributed in kind, the adjusted basis of this property must be fairly representative of the adjusted basis of all trust property available for distribution at the time of distribution. These provisions comply with section 1.664-3(a)(4) of the regulations The additional requirement that any such distribution be made only with the consent of Taxpayers is nor in conflict with these regulations. See section 3.04, Rev. Rul. 72-395, 1972-2 C.B. 340. Therefore, the authority of the trustee under paragraphs 8 and 21 of the trust instrument to make accelerated distributions to charity does not disqualify Trust as a charitable remainder unitrust, if it is otherwise qualified.

Paragraph 9 of the trust agreement allows the trustee to make a reasonable allocation to income from capital gains received by Trust on assets that produced limited or no income for the time Trust owned them.

Section 643(b) of the Code provides that, for purposes of this subpart and subparts B, C, and D, the term "income", when not preceded by the words "taxable", "distributable net", "undistributed net", or "gross", means the amount of income of the estate or trust for the taxable year determined under the terms of the governing instrument and applicable local law. Items of gross income constituting extraordinary dividends or taxable stock dividends which a fiduciary, acting in good faith, determines to be allocable to corpus under the terms of the governing instrument and applicable local law shall not be considered income.

The trustee's authority to allocate receipts and expenses between income and principal is governed by the State Principal and Income Act. In general, capital gains are allocated to principal. However, this act provides an exception:

A person making an outright gift or establishing a trust may make provision in the creating instrument for the manner of ascertainment of income and principal and the apportionment of receipts and expenditures or grant discretion to the personal representative or trustee to do so and the provision, where not otherwise contrary to law, controls notwithstanding sections 30-3101 to 30-3115.

Neb. Rev. Stat. section 30-3101 (Reissue 1989). Thus, a trustee in State may allocate capital gains on unproductive assets to income if the trust agreement specifically authorizes the trustee to do so. See In Re Johnson Trust, 320 N.W. 2d 466 (Neb. 1982).

Section 674(b)(8) of the Code provides that subsection (a) shall not apply to a power, regardless of by whom held, to allocate receipts and disbursements as between corpus and income, even though expressed in broad language.

The trust agreement provides for the allocation to income of some or all of the capital gains received by Trust on the sale or other disposition of any stock, bond, or other security that provided no or limited income during the period it was owned by Trust. This provision complies with section 674(b)(8) of the Code and is permitted by State law. Therefore, the authority of the trustee under paragraph 9 of the trust instrument to make reasonable allocations between income and principal of any gains from the disposition of unproductive assets does not disqualify Trust as a charitable remainder unitrust, if it is otherwise qualified.

RULING REQUEST 2

Paragraph 14 of the trust agreement appoints first Taxpayer A, then Taxpayer B, as the investment manager of Trust and gives the investment manager authority to direct the investment of trust assets (other than assets having no readily ascertainable market value). In his capacity as investment manager for Trust, Taxpayer A anticipates directing the substantial investment of trust assets in Partnership. Partnership interests are valued and withdrawable quarterly. With the exception of securities of controlled companies, the market value of the partnership assets are computed on the basis of objective standards. Securities of controlled companies are valued in good faith by the general partners, based upon their judgement. Unless the securities of controlled companies make up a significant share of Partnership assets, these assets will not be considered assets having no readily ascertainable value.

As a trust described in section 4947(a)(2) of the Code, Trust is subject to chapter 42 of the Code, including the following sections: section 4941, relating to taxes on self dealing; section 4943, relating to taxes on excess business holdings, except as provided in subsection (b)(3); section 4944, relating to investments which jeopardize charitable purposes, except as provided in subsection (b)(3); and section 4945, relating to taxes on taxable expenditures.

If Taxpayers are allowed a deduction under section 170 of the Code with respect to transfers to Trust, then sections 4943 and 4944 are not applicable to the Trust by virtue of section 4947(b)(3).

Taxpayers represent that they will never charge or accept any fees, charges, or other benefits from Trust in respect of their services as investment manager for Trust. Accordingly, these services come within the exception provided in section 4941(d)(2)(C) of the Code, which states that the furnishing of goods, services, or facilities by a disqualified person to a private foundation shall not be an act of self-dealing if the furnishing is without charge and if the goods, services, or facilities so furnished are used exclusively for section 501(c)(3) purposes. In the event that Taxpayers do receive compensation for their services in the future, it will not constitute an act of self-dealing as long as the amount thereof is reasonable. See section 4941(d)(2)(E) of the Code and sections 53.4941(d)-3(c), Example (2), and 53.4941(d)-2(c)(4) of the Foundation and Similar Excise Tax Regulations.

Section 4945(d)(5) of the Code provides that the term "taxable expenditure" means any amount paid or incurred by a private foundation for any purpose other than one specified in section 170(c)(2)(B). Section 53.4945-6(b)(1) of the regulations provides that the following types of expenditures ordinarily will not be treated as taxable expenditures under section 4945(d)(5): (i) expenditures to acquire investments entered into for the purpose of obtaining income or funds to be used in furtherance of purposes described in section 170(c)(2)(B); and

(ii) reasonable expenses with respect to these investments. Assuming that Trust will make such investments, then it should not incur any taxable expenditures under section 4945.

Section 512(b)(1) of the Code provides that dividend and interest income is excluded from the definition of "unrelated business taxable income." Assuming that the income generated by Trust's investment activity is passive in nature, then Trust, if it was subject to the unrelated trade or business provisions, would not have any unrelated business taxable income.

RULINGS

Based solely on the facts as presented in this ruling request, and viewed in light of the applicable law and regulations, we rule as follows.

(1) Except for paragraphs 14 and 15, the provisions of the trust agreement not contained in Rev. Proc. 90-31 (paragraphs 8, 9, 13, and 21), will not disqualify Trust as a charitable remainder unitrust under section 664 of the Code, if it is otherwise qualified. Regarding paragraphs 14 and 15 of the trust agreement, if the circumstances surrounding the administration of Trust indicate that either the investment manager or the independent investment manager holds a power of administration within the meaning of section 675(4) of the Code and that such a power is held in a nonfiduciary capacity, then Taxpayers will be treated as the owner of the entire Trust and Trust will not be deemed created for purposes of section 664. Thus, Trust would not qualify as a charitable remainder unitrust under section 664.

(2) The investment of trust assets in Partnership at the direction of Taxpayer A or B acting as the investment manager of Trust will not disqualify Trust as a charitable remainder unitrust under section 664 of the Code. However, if the circumstances surrounding the administration of Trust indicate that the investment manager holds a power of administration within the meaning of section 675(4) of the Code and that such a power is held in a nonfiduciary capacity, then Taxpayers will be treated as the owner of the entire Trust and Trust will not be deemed created for purposes of section 664. Thus, Trust would not qualify as a charitable remainder unitrust under section 664.

No opinion is expressed or implied as to any other provisions of the trust agreement or as to the federal tax consequences of the formation and operation of Trust under any other provisions of the Code. Specifically, no opinion is expressed as to whether Trust qualifies as a charitable remainder trust under section 664.

A copy of this letter should be attached to the federal income tax return of Taxpayers for the tax year in which Trust is formed. A copy of this letter is enclosed for that purpose.

In accordance with the power of attorney on file with this office, we are sending a copy of this letter to your authorized representative.

This ruling is directed only to the taxpayer who requested it According to section 6110(j)(3) of the Code, this ruling may not be cited or used as precedent.

9. For those interested is this controversial letter ruling, the full ruling states:

Code Sec. 664

* Sec. 664 Issues: Charitable remainder trusts — Definitions; Unitrust with income exception.

This responds to a letter from your authorized representative dated June 8, 1994, as supplemented and amended November 16, 1994, in which he asks us on your behalf to rule on the qualification of Trust as a charitable remainder unitrust under section 664 of the Internal Revenue Code and on the income and gift tax consequences of a transfer to Trust.

According to section 4.01(39) of Rev. Proc. 94-3, 1994-1 I.R.B. 79, the Service ordinarily will not rule on whether a charitable remainder trust that provides for annuity or unitrust payments for one or two measuring lives satisfies the requirements described in section 664 of the Code. In addition, according to sections 4.01(16), (44), and (46) of Rev. Proc. 94-3, the Service ordinarily will not rule on whether a transfer to a charitable remainder trust described in section 664 that provides for annuity or unitrust payments for one or two measuring lives qualifies for charitable deductions under sections 170(f)(2)(A), 2055(e)(2)(A), and 2522(c)(2)(A).

In lieu of seeking the Service's advance approval of a charitable remainder unitrust, taxpayers are directed to follow the sample provisions for charitable remainder unitrusts outlined in Rev. Proc. 90-31, 1990-1 C.B. 539. By following the models contained in Rev. Proc. 90-31, taxpayers can be assured that the Service will recognize a trust as meeting all of the requirements of a charitable remainder unitrust under section 664(d)(2) and (3), provided that the trust operates in a manner consistent with the terms of the trust instrument and provided it is a valid trust under applicable local law. For transfers to a qualifying charitable remainder unitrust, the present value of the remainder interest will be deductible under sections 170(f)(2)(A), 2055(e)(2) (A), and 2522(c)(2)(A) if the charitable beneficiary otherwise meets all of the requirements of these sections.

Pursuant to Rev. Proc. 94-3, the Service will not rule on whether Trust qualifies as a charitable remainder unitrust under section 664 of the Code or whether charitable income tax and gift tax deductions will be allowed to Taxpayer under sections 170 and 2522 for the present value of the remainder interest.

The trust agreement contains provisions, however, that are not included in, or are different from, the sample provisions outlined in Rev. Proc. 90-31. Paragraph x of the trust agreement directs the trustee to allocate realized capital gains to trust income. Paragraph y of the trust agreement provides for the accrual of the makeup amount as a liability in computing the unitrust amount. Therefore, we will rule on whether these provisions comply with the requirements for a charitable remainder unitrust under section 664 of the Code.

FACTS

Taxpayer will establish Trust, to be governed by the laws of State. Taxpayer will fund Trust in A with approximately $B of Company common stock. Taxpayer will be the initial trustee and the lifetime income beneficiary of Trust.

Foundation will be the charitable remainder beneficiary of Trust. Taxpayer is the trustee of Foundation.

Trust will distribute annually to Taxpayer an amount equal to the lesser of trust income for the tax year or 10 percent of the net fair market value of trust assets (determined as of the first day of each tax year of Trust). If trust income for the tax year is less than 10 percent of the fair market value of trust assets, the income shortfall will accumulate and be distributed in subsequent years when trust income exceeds 10 percent.

Paragraph X of the trust agreement provides that the trustee shall allocate to trust income all gains realized on trust assets after contribution to Trust (whether attributable to appreciation occurring before or after contribution).

In computing the unitrust amount for each year, the liability to the taxpayer resulting from any income shortfall will be taken into account. Paragraph y of the trust agreement provides that the net fair market value of the trust assets as of the valuation date is to be determined by first subtracting the amount of the shortfall as of that date, provided that the reduction is no more than the amount of the unrealized gain then inherent in the trust assets.

LAW & ANALYSIS

Section 664(d)(2) of the Code provides that, for purposes of this section, a charitable remainder unitrust is a trust —

    (A) from which a fixed percentage (which is not less than 5 percent) of the net fair market value of its assets, valued annually, is to be paid, not less often than annually, to one or more persons (at least one of which is not an organization described in section 170(c) and, in the case of individuals, only to an individual who is living at the time of the creation of the trust) for a term of years (not in excess of 20 years) or for the life or lives of such individual or individuals,

    (B) from which no amount other than the payments described in subparagraph (A) may be paid to or for the use of any person other than an organization described in section 170(c), and

    (C) following the termination of the payments described in subparagraph (A), the remainder interest in the trust is to be transferred to, or for the use of, an organization described in section 170(c) or is to be retained by the trust for such a use.

Section 664(d)(3) of the Code provides that, notwithstanding the provisions of paragraphs (2)(A) and (B), the trust instrument may provide that the trustee shall pay the income beneficiary for any year —

   (A) the amount of the trust income, if such amount is less than the amount required to be distributed under paragraph (2)(A), and

   (B) any amount of the trust income which is in excess of the amount required to be distributed under paragraph (2)(A), to the extent that (by reason of subparagraph (A)), the aggregate of the amounts paid in prior years was less than the aggregate of such required amounts.

Section 1.664-3(a)(1)(i)(b)(1) of the Income Tax Regulations provides that the amount of trust income for purposes of section 664(d)(3) of the Code is the amount of trust income as defined in section 643(b) and the regulations thereunder.

Section 643(b) of the Code provides that, for purposes of subparts A through D, part I, subchapter J, chapter 1, the term "income", when not preceded by the words "taxable", "distributable net", "undistributed net", or "gross", means the amount of income of the estate or trust for the taxable year determined under the terms of the governing instrument and applicable local law. Items of gross income constituting extraordinary dividends or taxable stock dividends which a fiduciary, acting in good faith, determines to be allocable to corpus under the terms of the governing instrument and applicable local law shall not be considered income.

Section 1.643(b)-1 of the regulations provides, however, that trust provisions which depart fundamentally from concepts of local law in the determination of what constitutes income are not recognized. For example, if a trust instrument directs that all the trust income shall be paid to A, but defines ordinary dividends and interest as corpus, the trust will not be considered one which under its governing instrument is required to distribute all its income currently for purposes of section 642(b) (relating to the personal exemption) and section 651 (relating to "simple" trusts).

Under State law, principal includes, but is not limited to, consideration received by the trustee on the sale or other transfer of principal. Cite 1. Thus, capital gains generally are allocated to principal under State law. However, State law allows the terms of the governing instrument to control the allocation of receipts and expenditures.

A trust shall be administered with due regard to the respective interests of the income beneficiaries and remainder beneficiaries. A trust is so administered with respect to the allocation of receipts and expenditures if a receipt is credited or an expenditure is charged to income or principal or partly to each in accordance with the terms of the trust notwithstanding contrary provisions of this chapter. Cite 2.

In the present situation, Trust's governing instrument provides that all gains realized on Trust's assets are to be allocated to trust income, and such an allocation is permitted under State law. Thus, under the terms of the governing instrument and applicable local law, the amount of trust income for purposes of the computations under section 664(d)(3) includes the appreciation in trust assets once the appreciation is realized by the sale or other disposition of those assets.

The unitrust amount determined under section 664(d)(2)(A) of the Code is a fixed percentage of the fair market value of the trust's assets valued annually. For a trust described in section 664(d)(2), the unitrust amount is paid each year to the noncharitable beneficiary. If the trust's income is insufficient to cover the unitrust amount, the principal must be invaded to make up any shortfall. Under these circumstances, the fair market value of the trust assets will decrease by the unitrust amount that was paid from principal. The unitrust amount for the subsequent years will be decreased accordingly.

The income exception provision of section 664(d)(3) was enacted by Congress to permit greater flexibility for certain charitable remainder gifts, but it was crafted in such a manner as to prevent the manipulation of the trust assets to the detriment of the charitable remainder interest. If the income exception provision is included in a trust's governing instrument, this provision prevents the trust from having to invade corpus when the income for the year is below what was originally contemplated. For purposes of this provision, the determination of what constitutes trust income is to be made under the applicable local law and, thus, is not to include items such as capital gains which must be allocated to the trust principal. S. Rep. No. 552, 91st Cong., 1st Sess. 87-89 (1969); reprinted 1969-3 C.B. 423, 480-481.

For a trust described in sections 664(d)(2) and (d)(3), the unitrust amount determined under section 664(d)(2)(A) is used as the ceiling for the amount payable to the noncharitable beneficiary each year and for the amount of any deficiency that may be made up in future years. Provided the trust income does not exceed the current year's unitrust amount and any deficiency from prior years, the trust income is paid out to the noncharitable beneficiary each year. As envisioned by Congress, the trust income used to pay the unitrust amount would never include amounts that in prior years had been included in the fair market value of the trust assets on which the fixed unitrust amount had been based.

The allocation of capital gains to trust income creates the potential to manipulate the trust assets to the detriment of the charitable remainder interest. Year after year, the trustee naturally includes any unrealized appreciation in determining the fair market value of the trust's assets on which the unitrust amount is based. Then when the trustee chooses to realize the appreciation by selling the assets, the realized appreciation is taken out of the base. The realized appreciation becomes trust income that will be paid to the noncharitable beneficiary to the extent of the current year's unitrust amount and any deficiency in the unitrust amounts from prior years. The trustee has, thus, inflated the unitrust amount each year by amounts that will be payable to the noncharitable beneficiary upon the sale of assets. Under these circumstances, the amount that will be paid to the charitable organization at the termination of the trust may well be less than the amount that would be paid to the charitable organization if the fixed unitrust were paid each year pursuant to section 664(d)(2)(A) of the Code.

The income exception of section 664(d)(3) of the Code may not be used in a manner that would allow the value of assets actually passing to the charitable organization to be less than it would have been under section 664(d)(2)(A). If under the terms of the governing instrument and applicable local law the trust's capital gains are allocated to trust income, then the trust's obligation to pay the prior years' deficiency to the noncharitable beneficiary must be accounted for to the extent that the trustee would trigger that obligation if he sold the assets on the valuation date.

Thus, in determining the fair market value of the assets on the annual valuation date, the governing instrument must require the trustee to treat as a liability the amount of any deficiency for prior years computed under section 664(d)(3)(B). The amount treated as a liability need not exceed the trust's unrealized appreciation that would be trust income under the terms of the governing instrument and applicable local law if the trustee sold all the assets in the trust on the valuation date. This trust provision will ensure that the timing of the realization of the gain by the trustee cannot be manipulated to the detriment of the charitable remainder interest.

In the present situation, all gains realized on the sale or other disposition of Trust's assets are allocated to trust income under the terms of the governing instrument and applicable local law. The governing instrument provides that for purposes of determining the unitrust amount each year, the fair market value of the assets shall be reduced by the amount of any deficiency in unitrust payments from prior years but such reduction shall not exceed the amount of the unrealized gain in Trust's assets as of the valuation date. Thus, because the trust provision allocating capital gains to trust income is coupled with a trust provision treating a specific amount of any unitrust deficiency as a liability in valuing the trust's assets, these provisions comply with the requirements for a charitable remainder unitrust described in section 664(d)(2) and (d)(3) of the Code and the regulations thereunder.

RULING

Based solely on the facts as presented in this ruling request, and viewed in light of the applicable law and regulations, we rule that Paragraphs x and y of the trust agreement comply with the requirements for a charitable remainder unitrust under section 664 of the Code.

No opinion is expressed or implied as to any other provisions of the trust agreement or as to the federal tax consequences of the formation and operation of Trust under any other provisions of the Code. Specifically, no opinion is expressed as to whether Trust otherwise qualifies as a charitable remainder trust under section 664

10. A charitable remainder interest in an irrevocable trust subject to invasion to make fixed payments to the life tenant is not deductible under section 2055 or 2522 of the Code (for gift or estate tax purposes) where the probability that the transfer will not occur is greater than five percent. This was set out under Rev. Rul 70-452 as follows:

REV. RUL. 70-452

Advice has been requested whether a deduction is allowable under section 2522 of the Internal Revenue Code of 1954 (prior to amendment by the Tax Reform Act of 1969, P.L. 91-172, C.B. 1969-3, 10) with respect to a remainder interest in a trust that is payable to charity under the circumstances described below. During 1968, a donor transferred property valued at $162,000 to an irrevocable trust. Under the terms of the trust agreement, the trustees are directed to pay to A, aged 62, all the trust income plus $6,000 of the trust principal each year during her lifetime. The trust is to terminate upon the death of A at which time the principal and any accumulated income is to be paid to a named charitable organization.

Where a portion of trust principal in addition to the income must be distributed periodically, the length of time the trust can exist is susceptible of calculation. A fund of $162,000 from which $6,000 is payable annually from principal will last for a period of 27 years. Based upon U.S. Life Table 38, prescribed by section 25.2512-5(e) of the Gift Tax Regulations, the probability that a person aged 62 will be alive 27 years hence is 0.072 or 7.2 percent.

Section 25.2522(a)-2(b) of the regulations provides that if, as of the date of the gift, a transfer for charitable purposes is dependent upon the performance of some act or the happening of a precedent event in order that it might become effective, no deduction is allowable unless the possibility that the charitable transfer will not become effective is so remote as to be negligible.

The charitable deduction is not allowable where the probability exceeds 5 percent that the noncharitable income beneficiary will survive the exhaustion of the fund in which charity has a remainder interest. Any possibility in excess of 5 percent that the contingency will occur and defeat charity's interest is not considered so remote as to be negligible within the meaning of the regulations. In this connection see sections 2037 and 2042 of the Code which specify that 5 percent is the value at which a reversionary interest will be considered significant. The charitable deduction was disallowed in Estate of George M. Moffett v. Commissioner, 269 F. 2d 738 (1959), where the probability that the fund would be exhausted was 19 percent and in United States v. Bertha Dean, 224 F. 2d 26 (1955), where the probability was 9 percent.

In the above-described circumstances, the probability that charity will not take is in excess of 5 percent. Accordingly, it is held that the charitable deduction is not allowable for the transfer in trust. Similarly, the estate tax charitable deduction is not allowable with respect to comparable testamentary transfers. Section 20.2055-2(b) of the Estate Tax Regulations.

This test exists for *annuity* trusts because the payment to the income beneficiaries is level throughout the life of the trust, making it possible to exhaust the trust corpus. Since a *unitrust* adjusts its payout to the income beneficiaries based on the increase or decrease of asset values, the exhaustion of trust corpus is unlikely.

Chapter 5

1. Self dealing is broadly defined by IRC §4941(d) as follows:

   (1) IN GENERAL

   For purposes of this section, the term "self-dealing" means any direct or indirect —

   (A) sale or exchange, or leasing, of property between a private foundation and a disqualified person;

   (B) lending of money or other extension of credit between a private foundation and a disqualified person;

   (C) furnishing of goods, services, or facilities between a private foundation and a disqualified person;

   (D) payment of compensation (or payment or reimbursement of expenses) by a private foundation to a disqualified person;

   (E) transfer to, or use by or for the benefit of, a disqualified person of the income or assets of a private foundation; and

   (F) agreement by a private foundation to make any payment of money or other property to a government official (as defined in section 4946(c)), other than an agreement to employ such individual for any period after the termination of his government service if such individual is terminating his government service within a 90-day period.

   Reg 53.4941(d)-2(d) gives examples as follows:

   (d) FURNISHING GOODS, SERVICES, OR FACILITIES —

   (1) IN GENERAL. Except as provided in subparagraph (2) or (3) of this paragraph (or Section 53.4941(d)-3(b)), the furnishing of goods, services, or facilities between a private foundation and a disqualified person shall constitute an act of self-dealing. This subparagraph shall apply, for example, to the furnishing of goods, services, or facilities such as office space, automobiles, auditoriums, secretarial help, meals, libraries, publications, laboratories, or parking lots. Thus, for example, if a foundation *furnishes personal living quarters* (emphasis added) to a disqualified person (other than a foundation manager or employee) without charge, such furnishing shall be an act of self-dealing.

2. The newly proposed section 664 regulations will alleviate one problem in that they will permit the donor-trustee to rely on an appraisal by a qualified appraiser as provided for by Section 170A for the valuation for trust income purposes. This eliminates the need to have an inde-

pendent trustee that values the hard-to-value assets, usually by referring to the aforementioned appraisal that is needed by the taxpayer for substantiation of the charitable income tax deduction.

3. Reg. 1.170A-13(c)(1) states:

(c) DEDUCTIONS IN EXCESS OF $5,000 FOR CERTAIN CHARITABLE CONTRIBUTIONS OF PROPERTY MADE AFTER DECEMBER 31, 1984 —

(1) GENERAL RULE —

> (i) IN GENERAL. This paragraph applies to any charitable contribution made after December 31, 1984, by an individual, closely held corporation, personal service corporation, partnership, or S corporation of an item of property (other than money and publicly traded securities to which Section 1.170A-13(c)(7)(xi)(B) does not apply if the amount claimed or reported as a deduction under section 170 with respect to such item exceeds $5,000. This paragraph also applies to charitable contributions by C corporations (as defined in section 1361(a)(2) of the Code) to the extent described in paragraph (c)(2)(ii) of this section. No deduction under section 170 shall be allowed with respect to a charitable contribution to which this paragraph applies unless the substantiation requirements described in paragraph (c)(2) of this section are met. For purposes of this paragraph (c), the amount claimed or reported as a deduction for an item of property is the aggregate amount claimed or reported as a deduction for a charitable contribution under section 170 or such items of property and all similar items of property (as defined in paragraph (c)(7)(iii) of this section) by the same donor for the same taxable year (whether or not donated to the same donee).

There is a great deal of misunderstanding about the requirements for this qualified appraisal. Some practitioners have opined that it is not needed if the property sold quickly, etc. However, the regulations are very detailed and specific in this area, and no such safe harbor exists. Reg. 1.170A-13(c)(3) deals with these requirements by stating:

(3) QUALIFIED APPRAISAL —

> (i) IN GENERAL. For purposes of this paragraph (c), the term "qualified appraisal" means an appraisal document that —

> (A) Relates to an appraisal that is made not earlier than 60 days prior to the date of contribution of the appraised property nor later than the date specified in paragraph (c) (3)(iv)(B) of this section;

> (B) Is prepared, signed, and dated by a qualified appraiser (within the meaning of paragraph (c)(5) of this section);

(C) Includes the information required by paragraph (c)(3)(ii) of this section; and

(D) Does not involve an appraisal fee prohibited by paragraph (c)(6) of this section.

    (ii) INFORMATION INCLUDED IN QUALIFIED APPRAISAL. A qualified appraisal shall include the following information:

(A) A description of the property in sufficient detail for a person who is not generally familiar with the type of property to ascertain that the property that was appraised is the property that was (or will be) contributed;

(B) In the case of tangible property, the physical condition of the property;

(C) The date (or expected date) of contribution to the donee;

(D) The terms of any agreement or understanding entered into (or expected to be entered into) by or on behalf of the donor or donee that relates to the use, sale, or other disposition of the property contributed, including, for example, the terms of any agreement or understanding that —

(1) Restricts temporarily or permanently a donee's right to use or dispose of the donated property,

(2) Reserves to, or confers upon, anyone (other than a donee organization or an organization participating with a donee organization in cooperative fundraising) any right to the income from the contributed property or to the possession of the property, including the right to vote donated securities, to acquire the property by purchase or otherwise, or to designate the person having such income, possession, or right to acquire, or

(3) Earmarks donated property for a particular use;

    (E) The name, address, and (if a taxpayer identification number is otherwise required by section 6109 and the regulations thereunder) the identifying number of the qualified appraiser; and, if the qualified appraiser is acting in his or her capacity as a partner in a partnership, an employee of any person (whether an individual, corporation, or partnerships), or an independent contractor engaged by a person other than the donor, the name, address, and taxpayer identification number (if a number is otherwise required by section 6109 and the regulations thereunder) of the partnership or the person who employs or engages the qualified appraiser;

    (F) The qualifications of the qualified appraiser who signs the appraisal, including the appraiser's background, experience, education, and membership, if any, in professional appraisal associations;

    (G) A statement that the appraisal was prepared for income tax purposes;

(H) The date (or dates) on which the property was appraised;
(I) The appraised fair market value (within the meaning of Section 1.170A-1(c)(2)) of the property on the date (or expected date) of contribution;
(J) The method of valuation used to determine the fair market value, such as the income approach, the market-data approach, and the replacement-cost-less-depreciation approach; and
(K) The specific basis for the valuation, such as specific comparable sales transactions or statistical sampling, including a justification for using sampling and an explanation of the sampling procedure employed.

    (iii) EFFECT OF SIGNATURE OF THE QUALIFIED APPRAISER. Any appraiser who falsely or fraudulently overstates the value of the contributed property referred to in a qualified appraisal or appraisal summary (as defined in paragraphs (c)(3) and (4), respectively, of this section) that the appraiser has signed may be subject to a civil penalty under section 6701 for aiding and abetting an understatement of tax liability and, moreover, may have appraisals disregarded pursuant to 31 U.S.C. 330(c).

    (iv) SPECIAL RULES —

(A) NUMBER OF QUALIFIED APPRAISALS. For purposes of paragraph (c)(2)(i)(A) of this section, a separate qualified appraisal is required for each item of property that is not included in a group of similar items of property. See paragraph (c)(7)(iii) of this section for the definition of similar items of property. Only one qualified appraisal is required for a group of similar items of property contributed in the same taxable year of the donor, although a donor may obtain separate qualified appraisals for each item of property. A qualified appraisal prepared with respect to a group of similar items of property shall provide all the information required by paragraph (c)(3)(ii) of this section for each item of similar property, except that the appraiser may select any items whose aggregate value is appraised at $100 or less and provide a group description of such items.

(B) TIME OF RECEIPT OF QUALIFIED APPRAISAL. The qualified appraisal must be received by the donor before the due date (including extensions) of the return on which a deduction is first claimed (or reported in the case of a donor that is a partnership or S corporation) under section 170 with respect to the donated property, or, in the case of a deduction first claimed (or reported) on an amended return, the date on which the return is filed.

For more general information on qualified appraisals for charitable gifts see Keligian, John, "Appraisal issues now require greater attention for tax planning to be effective"., Vol. 80, *Journal of Taxation*, 02-01-1994, pp 98.

Chapter 6

1. Here is an illustration of benefits on a year-by-year basis. The assumed investment rate of return is 9 percent, made up of 2 percent ordinary income and 7 percent long term capital gain income.

Comparison of Benefits
Anthony and Linda Wright

A. Input Assumptions:		
	#1	#2
Type of Technique	Sell Invest.	Unitrust-Std
Time Period Projected	1997-2020	1997-2020
Income Payout Rate	All Income	6.00%
Income is Paid	Quarterly	Quarterly
Investment Period Measured by	2 Lives	2 Lives
B. Contributions:		
Fair Market Value of Property	$900,000	$900,000
Income Tax Deduction Permitted	0	219,463
Capital Gains Tax on Sale	246,500	0
C. Cash Flow:		
After Tax Income During Life	$948,804	$1,324,946
D. Estate for Heirs:		
Gross Value of Estate	$653,500	0
(+) Life Insurance Death Benefit	0	0
(–) Estate Taxes	326,750	0
(=) Net Estate for Heirs	326,750	0
E. Benefit Summary:		
Net Income + Net Estate		
equals Total Family Benefit	1,275,554	1,324,946
(+) Endowment to Charity	0	1,746,066
(=) Total Benefit	1,275,554	3,071,012

This proforma should not be assumed to predict any future investment results, nor does it take into consideration possible tax changes.
PLEASE CONSULT YOUR ATTORNEY FOR ALL LEGAL MATTERS.

Comparison of Net Spendable Income (After Tax)
Anthony and Linda Wright

Yr	Sell #1	6 % StdCRUT
1	39,533	49,852
2	39,533	51,054
3	39,533	52,290
4	39,533	53,561
5	39,533	54,867
6	39,533	56,209
7	39,533	43,795
8	39,533	45,021
9	39,533	46,281
10	39,533	47,577
11	39,533	48,909
12	39,533	50,279
13	39,533	51,686
14	39,533	53,134
15	39,533	54,621
16	39,533	56,151
17	39,533	57,723
18	39,533	59,339
19	39,533	61,000
20	39,533	62,708
21	39,533	64,464
22	39,533	66,269
23	39,533	68,124
24	39,533	70,032
Totals	948,804	1,324,946

Comparison of Value of Assets
Anthony and Linda Wright

Yr	Sell #1	6 % StdCRUT
1	653,500	925,199
2	653,500	951,103
3	653,500	977,732
4	653,500	1,005,107
5	653,500	1,033,248
6	653,500	1,062,177
7	653,500	1,091,917
8	653,500	1,122,489
9	653,500	1,153,916
10	653,500	1,186,224
11	653,500	1,219,436
12	653,500	1,253,579
13	653,500	1,288,677

14	653,500	1,324,758
15	653,500	1,361,849
16	653,500	1,399,978
17	653,500	1,439,175
18	653,500	1,479,470
19	653,500	1,520,893
20	653,500	1,563,475
21	653,500	1,607,250
22	653,500	1,652,250
23	653,500	1,698,511
24	653,500	1,746,066

Chapter 7

1. The tax rate applied to long term capital gains has gone up and down over the years. In the most recent move in 1997 the rate was once again reduced to a maximum of 20 percent. Historically, even when the rate was 20 percent, people have had an adverse reaction to paying the tax because the sheer magnitude of the tax on large gains is unpalatable to many people. It is an emotional issue, and people often fail to make good decisions when they are driven by emotions.

2. The IRS issued a letter ruling that has generated a great deal of discussion by professionals who practice in this area. They attempted to rule that the accumulated makeup account should be considered a "liability" of the trust when calculating the amount to be paid to income recipients. The affect of this ruling, if accurate, would eliminate part of the "compounding" of makeup available from the trust. It also dealt with the ability to use a limited partnership format to control the flow of net income. As this is an important ruling to understand, the full text is as follows:

* Sec. 664 Issues: Charitable remainder trusts — Definitions; Unitrust with income exception.

This responds to a letter from your authorized representative dated June 8, 1994, as supplemented and amended November 16, 1994, in which he asks us on your behalf to rule on the qualification of Trust as a charitable remainder unitrust under section 664 of the Internal Revenue Code and on the income and gift tax consequences of a transfer to Trust.

According to section 4.01(39) of Rev. Proc. 94-3, 1994-1 I.R.B. 79, the Service ordinarily will not rule on whether a charitable remainder trust that provides for annuity or unitrust payments for one or two measuring lives satisfies the requirements described in section 664 of the Code. In addition, according to sections 4.01(16), (44), and (46) of Rev. Proc. 94-3, the Service ordinarily will not rule on whether a transfer to a charitable remainder trust described in section 664 that provides for annuity or unitrust payments for one or two measuring lives qualifies for charitable deductions under sections 170(f)(2)(A),

2055(e)(2)(A), and 2522(c)(2)(A).

In lieu of seeking the Service's advance approval of a charitable remainder unitrust, taxpayers are directed to follow the sample provisions for charitable remainder unitrusts outlined in Rev. Proc. 90-31, 1990-1 C.B. 539. By following the models contained in Rev. Proc. 90-31, taxpayers can be assured that the Service will recognize a trust as meeting all of the requirements of a charitable remainder unitrust under section 664(d)(2) and (3), provided that the trust operates in a manner consistent with the terms of the trust instrument and provided it is a valid trust under applicable local law. For transfers to a qualifying charitable remainder unitrust, the present value of the remainder interest will be deductible under sections 170(f)(2)(A), 2055(e)(2)(A), and 2522(c)(2)(A) if the charitable beneficiary otherwise meets all of the requirements of these sections.

Pursuant to Rev. Proc. 94-3, the Service will not rule on whether Trust qualifies as a charitable remainder unitrust under section 664 of the Code or whether charitable income tax and gift tax deductions will be allowed to Taxpayer under sections 170 and 2522 for the present value of the remainder interest.

The trust agreement contains provisions, however, that are not included in, or are different from, the sample provisions outlined in Rev. Proc. 90-31. Paragraph x of the trust agreement directs the trustee to allocate realized capital gains to trust income. Paragraph y of the trust agreement provides for the accrual of the makeup amount as a liability in computing the unitrust amount. Therefore, we will rule on whether these provisions comply with the requirements for a charitable remainder unitrust under section 664 of the Code.

FACTS

Taxpayer will establish Trust, to be governed by the laws of State. Taxpayer will fund Trust in A with approximately $B of Company common stock. Taxpayer will be the initial trustee and the lifetime income beneficiary of Trust.

Foundation will be the charitable remainder beneficiary of Trust. Taxpayer is the trustee of Foundation.

Trust will distribute annually to Taxpayer an amount equal to the lesser of trust income for the tax year or 10 percent of the net fair market value of trust assets (determined as of the first day of each tax year of Trust). If trust income for the tax year is less than 10 percent of the fair market value of trust assets, the income shortfall will accumulate and be distributed in subsequent years when trust income exceeds 10 percent.

Paragraph x of the trust agreement provides that the trustee shall allocate to trust income all gains realized on trust assets after contribution to Trust (whether attributable to appreciation occurring before or after contribution).

In computing the unitrust amount for each year, the liability to the taxpayer resulting from any income shortfall will be taken into account. Paragraph y of the trust agreement provides that the net fair market value of the trust assets as of the valuation date is to be determined by first subtracting the amount of the shortfall as of that date, provided that the reduction is no more than the amount of the unrealized gain then inherent in the trust assets.

LAW & ANALYSIS

Section 664(d)(2) of the Code provides that, for purposes of this section, a charitable remainder unitrust is a trust —

(A) from which a fixed percentage (which is not less than 5 percent) of the net fair market value of its assets, valued annually, is to be paid, not less often than annually, to one or more persons (at least one of which is not an organization described in section 170(c) and, in the case of individuals, only to an individual who is living at the time of the creation of the trust) for a term of years (not in excess of 20 years) or for the life or lives of such individual or individuals,

(B) from which no amount other than the payments described in subparagraph (A) may be paid to or for the use of any person other than an organization described in section 170(c), and

(C) following the termination of the payments described in subparagraph (A), the remainder interest in the trust is to be transferred to, or for the use of, an organization described in section 170(c) or is to be retained by the trust for such a use.

Section 664(d)(3) of the Code provides that, notwithstanding the provisions of paragraphs (2)(A) and (B), the trust instrument may provide that the trustee shall pay the income beneficiary for any year —

(A) the amount of the trust income, if such amount is less than the amount required to be distributed under paragraph (2)(A), and

(B) any amount of the trust income which is in excess of the amount required to be distributed under paragraph (2)(A), to the extent that (by reason of subparagraph (A)), the aggregate of the amounts paid in prior years was less than the aggregate of such required amounts.

Section 1.664-3(a)(1)(i)(b)(1) of the Income Tax Regulations provides that the amount of trust income for purposes of section 664(d)(3) of the Code is the amount of trust income as defined in section 643(b) and the regulations thereunder.

Section 643(b) of the Code provides that, for purposes of subparts A through D, part I, subchapter J, chapter 1, the term "income", when not preceded by the words "taxable", "distributable net", "undistributed net", or "gross", means the amount of income of the estate or trust for the taxable year determined under the terms of the governing instrument and applicable local law. Items of gross income constituting extraordinary dividends or taxable stock dividends which a fiduciary, acting in good faith, determines to be allocable to corpus under the terms of the governing instrument and applicable local law shall not be considered income.

Section 1.643(b)-1 of the regulations provides, however, that trust provisions which depart fundamentally from concepts of local law in the determination of what constitutes income are not recognized. For example, if a trust instrument directs that all the trust income shall be paid to A, but defines ordinary dividends and interest as corpus, the trust will not be considered one which under its governing instrument is required to distribute all its income currently for purposes of section 642(b) (relating to the personal exemption) and section 651 (relating to "simple" trusts).

Under State law, principal includes, but is not limited to, consideration received by the trustee on the sale or other transfer of principal. Cite 1. Thus, capital gains generally are allocated to principal under State law. However, State law allows the terms of the governing instrument to control the allocation of receipts and expenditures.

A trust shall be administered with due regard to the respective interests of the income beneficiaries and remainder beneficiaries. A trust is so administered with respect to the allocation of receipts and expenditures if a receipt is credited or an expenditure is charged to income or principal or partly to each in accordance with the terms of the trust notwithstanding contrary provisions of this chapter. Cite 2.

In the present situation, Trust's governing instrument provides that all gains realized on Trust's assets are to be allocated to trust income, and such an allocation is permitted under State law. Thus, under the terms of the governing instrument and applicable local law, the amount of trust income for purposes of the computations under section 664(d)(3) includes the appreciation in trust assets once the appreciation is realized by the sale or other disposition of those assets.

The unitrust amount determined under section 664(d)(2)(A) of the Code is a fixed percentage of the fair market value of the trust's assets valued annually. For a trust described in section 664(d)(2), the unitrust amount is paid each year to the noncharitable beneficiary. If the trust's income is insufficient to cover the unitrust amount, the principal must be invaded to make up any shortfall. Under these circumstances, the fair market value of the trust assets will decrease by the unitrust amount that was paid from principal. The unitrust amount for the subsequent years will be decreased accordingly.

The income exception provision of section 664(d)(3) was enacted by Congress to permit greater flexibility for certain charitable remainder gifts, but it was crafted in such a manner as to prevent the manipulation of the trust assets to the detriment of the charitable remainder interest. If the income exception provision is included in a trust's governing instrument, this provision prevents the trust from having to invade corpus when the income for the year is below what was originally contemplated. For purposes of this provision, the determination of what constitutes trust income is to be made under the applicable local law and, thus, is not to include items such as capital gains which must be allocated to the trust principal. S. Rep. No. 552, 91st Cong., 1st Sess. 87-89 (1969); reprinted 1969-3 C.B. 423, 480-481.

For a trust described in sections 664(d)(2) and (d)(3), the unitrust amount determined under section 664(d)(2)(A) is used as the ceiling for the amount payable to the noncharitable beneficiary each year and for the amount of any deficiency that may be made up in future years. Provided the trust income does not exceed the current year's unitrust amount and any deficiency from prior years, the trust income is paid out to the noncharitable beneficiary each year. As envisioned by Congress, the trust income used to pay the unitrust amount would never include amounts that in prior years had been included in the fair market value of the trust assets on which the fixed unitrust amount had been based.

The allocation of capital gains to trust income creates the potential to manipulate the trust assets to the detriment of the charitable remainder interest. Year after year, the trustee naturally includes any unrealized appreciation in determining the fair market value of the trust's assets on which the unitrust amount is based. Then when the trustee chooses to realize the appreciation by selling the assets, the realized appreciation is taken out of the base. The realized appreciation becomes trust income that will be paid to the noncharitable beneficiary to the extent of the current year's unitrust amount and any deficiency in the unitrust amounts from prior years. The trustee has, thus, inflated the unitrust amount each year by amounts that will be payable to the noncharitable beneficiary upon the sale of assets. Under these circumstances, the amount that will be paid to the charitable organization at the termination of the trust may well be less than the amount that would be paid to the charitable organization if the fixed unitrust were paid each year pursuant to section 664(d)(2)(A) of the Code.

The income exception of section 664(d)(3) of the Code may not be used in a manner that would allow the value of assets actually passing to the charitable organization to be less than it would have been under section 664(d)(2)(A). If under the terms of the governing instrument and applicable local law the trust's capital gains are allocated to trust income, then the trust's obligation to pay the prior years' deficiency to the noncharitable beneficiary must be accounted for to the extent that the trustee would trigger that obligation if he sold the assets on the valuation date.

Thus, in determining the fair market value of the assets on the annual valuation date, the governing instrument must require the trustee to treat as a liability the amount of any deficiency for prior years computed under section 664(d)(3)(B). The amount treated as a liability need not exceed the trust's unrealized appreciation that would be trust income under the terms of the governing instrument and applicable local law if the trustee sold all the assets in the trust on the valuation date. This trust provision will ensure that the timing of the realization of the gain by the trustee cannot be manipulated to the detriment of the charitable remainder interest.

In the present situation, all gains realized on the sale or other disposition of Trust's assets are allocated to trust income under the terms of the governing instrument and applicable local law. The governing instrument provides that for purposes of determining the unitrust amount each year, the fair market value of the assets shall be reduced by the amount of any deficiency in unitrust payments from prior years but such reduction shall not exceed the amount of the unrealized gain in Trust's assets as of the valuation date. Thus, because the trust provision allocating capital gains to trust income is coupled with a trust provision treating a specific amount of any unitrust deficiency as a liability in valuing the trust's assets, these provisions comply with the requirements for a charitable remainder unitrust described in section 664(d)(2) and (d)(3) of the Code and the regulations thereunder.

RULING

Based solely on the facts as presented in this ruling request, and viewed in light of the applicable law and regulations, we rule that Paragraphs x and y of the trust agreement comply with the requirements for a charitable remainder unitrust under section 664 of the Code.

No opinion is expressed or implied as to any other provisions of the trust agreement or as to the federal tax consequences of the formation and operation of Trust under any other provisions of the Code. Specifically, no opinion is expressed as to whether Trust otherwise qualifies as a charitable remainder trust under section 664.

A copy of this letter should be attached to Taxpayer's federal income tax return for the tax year in which Trust is formed. A copy of this letter is enclosed for that purpose.

In accordance with the power of attorney on file with this office, we are sending copies of this letter to your authorized representatives.

This ruling is directed only to the taxpayer who requested it. According to section 6110(j)(3) of the Code, this ruling may not be cited or used as precedent.

Sincerely,
FRANCES D. SCHAFER
Senior Technician Reviewer,
Branch 3

3. In April, 1997 the IRS issued proposed regulations covering charitable remainder trusts, and as a part of the proposal they requested input from practitioners and others regarding what the service sees as an abuse of the net income provisions. Public hearings were held November, 1997, after which the IRS hopes to issue future guidance on how

this can be done within the parameters of the law. However, given some of the provisions of TRA '97 affecting CRTs, the IRS appears to be less concerned with this narrow, yet complex issue. Many top charitable tax-planning attorneys believe the ability to "time" the receipt of trust income can only be restricted through new legislation, none of which is even proposed. On January 9, 1998, the Service issued a Technical Advice Memorandum that permitted the use of this type of NIMCRUT funded by deferred annuities. If you are considering this type of trust, it is important to contact competent legal counsel.

4. There is currently a concern about the abuses that may result for the donors manipulating the trust to turn income on and off. There are very technical arguments on both sides, but the fact remains that care must be taken in this area. A solution that appears to work is the appointment of an "independent special trustee (IST)" to deal with the issues surrounding the deferral or payment of income. This is only needed when the donors are the regular trustees of the trust. An IST does not need to have any special talent, but must become informed about the working of the trust, the rights of the income and charitable beneficiaries, etc. This is really a fairly simple job, and hopefully the "rules" will be clarified. Since the maximum the income beneficiaries can receive is determined by the trust document, it is only the timing of the receipt of the income that is at issue.

Chapter 10

1. There is a significant amount of case law in the area of reasonable compensation. Under IRC §162(a) a deduction is allowable for "reasonable compensation." If a shareholder-employee's compensation is disallowed as a deduction by the Service, it becomes a non-deductible dividend to the corporation, still taxable to the employee.

2. The problem is that Joe is unlikely to meet the requirements of IRC § 302 for either a complete or substantially disproportionate redemption due to the family attribution rules of IRC§ 318. Without qualifying under §302, the partial redemption of stock would be considered a dividend under § 301.

3. See Note 37

4. Self-Dealing is defined in IRC§4941(d)(1) as follows:

(d) SELF-DEALING

    (1) IN GENERAL

For purposes of this section, the term "self-dealing" means any direct or indirect —

        (A) sale or exchange, or leasing, of property between a private foundation and a disqualified person;

        (B) lending of money or other extension of credit between a private foundation and a disqualified person;

        (C) furnishing of goods, services, or facilities between a private foundation and a disqualified person;

(D) payment of compensation (or payment or reimbursement of expenses) by a private foundation to a disqualified person;

(E) transfer to, or use by or for the benefit of, a disqualified person of the income or assets of a private foundation; and

(F) agreement by a private foundation to make any payment of money or other property to a government official (as defined in section 4946(c)), other than an agreement to employ such individual for any period after the termination of his government service if such individual is terminating his government service within a 90-day period.

5. When a donor is contributing part of the stock he owns in a closely held business it is likely that he and the corporation will be disqualified persons. This will cause most transactions like this to be structured to avoid being classified as self-dealing transactions. IRC 4946 provides:

SECTION 4946. DEFINITIONS AND SPECIAL RULES

(a) DISQUALIFIED PERSON

(1) IN GENERAL

For purposes of this subchapter, the term "disqualified person" means, with respect to a private foundation, a person who is —

(A) a substantial contributor to the foundation,

(B) a foundation manager (within the meaning of subsection (b)(1)),

(C) an owner of more than 20 percent of —
   (i)   the total combined voting power of a corporation,
   (ii) the profits interest of a partnership, or
   (iii) the beneficial interest of a trust or unincorporated enterprise, which is a substantial contributor to the foundation,

(D) a member of the family (as defined in subsection (d)) of any individual described in subparagraph (A), (B), or (C),

(E) a corporation of which persons described in subparagraph (A), (B), (C), or (D) own more than 35 percent of the total combined voting power,

(F) a partnership in which persons described in subparagraph (A), (B), (C), or (D) own more than 35 percent of the profits interest,

(G) a trust or estate in which persons described in subparagraph (A), (B), (C), or (D) hold more than 35 percent of the beneficial interest,

(H) only for purposes of section 4943, a private foundation —
   (i)   which is effectively controlled (directly or indirectly) by the same person or persons who control the private foundation in question, or
   (ii) substantially all of the contributions to which were made (directly or indirectly) by the same person or persons described in subparagraph (A), (B), or (C), or

members of their families (within the meaning of subsection (d)), who made (directly or indirectly) substantially all of the contributions to the private foundation in question, and

 (I) only for purposes of section 4941, a government official (as defined in subsection (c)).

(2) SUBSTANTIAL CONTRIBUTORS

For purposes of paragraph (1), the term "substantial contributor" means a person who is described in section 507(d)(2).

(3) STOCKHOLDINGS

For purposes of paragraphs (1)(C)(i) and (1)(E), there shall be taken into account indirect stockholdings which would be taken into account under section 267(c), except that, for purposes of this paragraph, section 267(c)(4) shall be treated as providing that the members of the family of an individual are the members within the meaning of subsection (d).

(4) PARTNERSHIPS; TRUSTS

For purposes of paragraphs (1)(C)(ii) and (iii), (1)(F), and (1)(G), the ownership of profits or beneficial interests shall be determined in accordance with the rules for constructive ownership of stock provided in section 267(c) (other than paragraph (3) thereof), except that section 267(c)(4) shall be treated as providing that the members of the family of an individual are the members within the meaning of subsection (d).

(b) FOUNDATION MANAGER

For purposes of this subchapter, the term "foundation manager" means, with respect to any private foundation —

(1) an officer, director, or trustee of a foundation (or an individual having powers or responsibilities similar to those of officers, directors, or trustees of the foundation), and

(2) with respect to any act (or failure to act), the employees of the foundation having authority or responsibility with respect to such act (or failure to act).

(c) omitted

(d) MEMBERS OF FAMILY

For purposes of subsection (a)(1), the family of any individual shall include only his spouse, ancestors, children, grandchildren, great grandchildren, and the spouses of children, grandchildren, and great grandchildren.

6. IRC §4941(d)(2)(F)

Chapter 12

1. Reg. 20.2031-1(b) VALUATION OF PROPERTY IN GENERAL. The value of every item of property includible in a decedent's gross estate under sections 2031 through 2044 is its fair market value at the time of the decedent's death, except that if the executor elects the al-

ternate valuation method under section 2032, it is the fair market value thereof at the date, and with the adjustments, prescribed in that section. The fair market value is the price at which the property would change hands between a willing buyer and a willing seller, neither being under any compulsion to buy or to sell and both having reasonable knowledge of relevant facts. The fair market value of a particular item of property includible in the decedent's gross estate is not to be determined by a forced sale price. Nor is the fair market value of an item of property to be determined by the sale price of the item in a market other than that in which such item is most commonly sold to the public, taking into account the location of the item wherever appropriate. Thus, in the case of an item of property includible in the decedent's gross estate, which is generally obtained by the public in the retail market, the fair market value of such an item of property is the price at which the item or a comparable item would be sold at retail. For example, the fair market value of an automobile (an article generally obtained by the public in the retail market) includible in the decedent's gross estate is the price for which an automobile of the same or approximately the same description, make, model, age, condition, etc., could be purchased by a member of the general public and not the price for which the particular automobile of the decedent would be purchased by a dealer in used automobiles. Examples of items of property which are generally sold to the public at retail may be found in Sections 20.2031-6 and 20.2031-8. The value is generally to be determined by ascertaining as a basis the fair market value as of the applicable valuation date of each unit of property. For example, in the case of shares of stock or bonds, such unit of property is generally a share of stock or a bond. Livestock, farm machinery, harvested and growing crops must generally be itemized and the value of each item separately returned. Property shall not be returned at the value at which it is assessed for local tax purposes unless that value represents the fair market value as of the applicable valuation date. All relevant facts and elements of value as of the applicable valuation date shall be considered in every case. The value of items of property which were held by the decedent for sale in the course of a business generally should be reflected in the value of the business. For valuation of interests in businesses, see Section 20.2031-3. See Section 20.2031-2 and Sections 20.2031-4 through 20.2031-8 for further information concerning the valuation of other particular kinds of property. For certain circumstances under which the sale of an item of property at a price below its fair market value may result in a deduction for the estate, see paragraph (d)(2)of Section 20.2053-3. Reg 20.2031-1(b) Reg 20.2031-1(b).

Since the definition is imprecise because the "relevant facts" in each situation are so different, this has been fertile ground for planners, but has also been an area that has been hard fought by the IRS.

2. "If a donor transfers shares in a corporation to each of the donor's chil-

dren, the factor of corporate control in the family is not considered in valuing each transferred interest for purposes of section 2512 of the Code. For estate and gift tax valuation purposes, the Service will follow Bright, Propstra, Andrews, and Lee in not assuming that all voting power held by family members may be aggregated for purposes of determining whether the transferred shares should be valued as part of a controlling interest. Consequently, a minority discount will not be disallowed solely because a transferred interest, when aggregated with interests held by family members, would be a part of a controlling interest. This would be the case whether the donor held 100 percent or some lesser percentage of the stock immediately before the gift." Rev Rul 93-12, 1993-1 C.B. 202 In 1981 the IRS lost in the Fifth Circuit case of *Estate of Bright v U.S.*, 658 F.2d 999, but refused to concede the issue of minority discounts in family corporations. After losing a string of additional cases, the Service finally reversed its position and issued Rev Rul 93-12. See also, James R. Hitchner and Gary Roland, *Marketability and Control Govern Value of Family Business Taxation for Accountants.* January, 1994. Pg. 24

3. Perhaps the seminal case in the family limited partnership area, the *Harrison* case (Estate Of Daniel J. Harrison, Jr., et al v Commissioner T.C. Memo 1987-8) set the tone for things to come. The court, siding with the Harrison estate, found the value of FLP interests in the estate to be $33 million, rather than the $59.5 million asserted by the IRS. The court approached the problem by stating:

"Brief as is the instant of death, the court must pinpoint its valuation at this instant — the moment of truth, when the ownership of the decedent ends and the ownership of the successor begins. It is a fallacy, therefore, to argue value before — or — after death on the notion that valuation must be determined by the value either of the interest that ceases or of the interest that begins. Instead, the valuation is Determined by the interest that passes and the value of the interest Before or after death is pertinent only as it serves to indicate the value at death."

4. In 1990 Congress created a whole new chapter of the Internal Revenue Code (Chapter 14) to deal with value-shifting arrangements that were considered abusive, including various corporate and partnership "freeze" techniques. This is an extremely complex area of the Code that has a number of land mines for the unaware or inexperienced practitioner. It also becomes intertwined with state law issues. A number of highly respected specialist in the area feel that including a charity (or other non-family member) as a limited partner will increase the probability of maximizing the discount without running afoul of the Chapter 14 restrictions.

5. The issue of valuation is critical to many aspects of advanced wealth transfer planning. If the discounts are significant and the total values large, there can be excess taxes, interest, and possible penalties to pay. Along these lines, it becomes important to anticipate IRS challenge to the valuation discount and plan accordingly. One way that this can

be accomplished is to make the gifts or sales a "defined value." The transfer to the children is for $x of partnership units, with any excess going to charity. If the IRS determines a higher value per unit, the excess units go to charity. Not only would the IRS collect no excess gift tax, but the parents would receive additional charitable income tax deductions. This technique, and variations of it, are beyond the scope of this book.

Chapter 13

1. This is an area of significant concern in the design an implementation of life insurance trusts. It is not as simple as it may appear to set up a trust for children (and possibly grandchildren) that will allow the withdrawal of up to $20,000 per beneficiary ($10,000 from each spouse). An attorney experienced in drafting life insurance trusts should be used and all the gift tax and estate tax issues should be discussed. Where grandchildren are also involved the attorney should also be well-versed with the implications of the generation skipping rules. The I.R.S. has been active in this area, but have continued to lose in its efforts to tighten the rules. A good article is Labella and Avidon, *Crummey Powers Survive Attack by IRS: A Test Case Journal of the American Society of CLU & ChFC*, September, 1997.

Chapter 14

1. The statutory structure of a GRAT was established by section 2702. In order to qualify, the provisions of this section must be met. The QPRT, as described later, is actually of form of GRAT using a personal residence.
SECTION 2702. SPECIAL VALUATION RULES IN CASE OF TRANSFERS OF INTERESTS IN TRUSTS
(a) VALUATION RULES
(1) IN GENERAL
Solely for purposes of determining whether a transfer of an interest in trust to (or for the benefit of) a member of the transferor's family is a gift (and the value of such transfer), the value of any interest in such trust retained by the transferor or any applicable family member (as defined in section 2701(e)(2)) shall be determined as provided in paragraph (2).
(2) VALUATION OF RETAINED INTERESTS
    (A) IN GENERAL
The value of any retained interest which is not a qualified interest shall be treated as being zero.
    (B) VALUATION OF QUALIFIED INTEREST
The value of any retained interest which is a qualified interest shall be determined under section 7520.
(3) EXCEPTIONS

(A) IN GENERAL

This subsection shall not apply to any transfer —

    (i)   if such transfer is an incomplete gift,

    (ii) if such transfer involves the transfer of an interest in trust all the property in which consists of a residence to be used as a personal residence by persons holding term interests in such trust, or

    (iii) to the extent that regulations provide that such transfer is not inconsistent with the purposes of this section.

(B) INCOMPLETE GIFT

For purposes of subparagraph (A), the term "incomplete gift" means any transfer which would not be treated as a gift whether or not consideration was received for such transfer.

(b) QUALIFIED INTEREST

For purposes of this section, the term "qualified interest" means —

(1) any interest which consists of the right to receive fixed amounts payable not less frequently than annually,

(2) any interest which consists of the right to receive amounts which are payable not less frequently than annually and are a fixed percentage of the fair market value of the property in the trust (determined annually), and

(3) any noncontingent remainder interest if all of the other interests in the trust consist of interests described in paragraph (1) or (2).

(c) CERTAIN PROPERTY TREATED AS HELD IN TRUST

For purposes of this section —

(1) IN GENERAL

The transfer of an interest in property with respect to which there is 1 or more term interests shall be treated as a transfer of an interest in a trust.

(2) JOINT PURCHASES

If 2 or more members of the same family acquire interests in any property described in paragraph (1) in the same transaction (or a series of related transactions), the person (or persons) acquiring the term interests in such property shall be treated as having acquired the entire property and then transferred to the other persons the interests acquired by such other persons in the transaction (or series of transactions). Such transfer shall be treated as made in exchange for the consideration (if any) provided by such other persons for the acquisition of their interests in such property.

(3) TERM INTEREST

The term "term interest" means —

    (A) a life interest in property, or

    (B) an interest in property for a term of years.

(4) VALUATION RULE FOR CERTAIN TERM INTERESTS

If the nonexercise of rights under a term interest in tangible property would not have a substantial effect on the valuation of the remainder interest in such property —

(A) subparagraph (A) of subsection (a)(2) shall not apply to such term interest, and

(B) the value of such term interest for purposes of applying subsection (a)(1) shall be the amount which the holder of the term interest establishes as the amount for which such interest could be sold to an unrelated third party.

(d) TREATMENT OF TRANSFERS OF INTERESTS IN PORTION OF TRUST

In the case of a transfer of an income or remainder interest with respect to a specified portion of the property in a trust, only such portion shall be taken into account in applying this section to such transfer.

(e) MEMBER OF THE FAMILY

For purposes of this section, the term "member of the family" shall have the meaning given such term by section 2704(c)(2).

2. The GRAT generally pays a fixed number of dollars which translates to a percentage of the assets. It may be desirable when transferring "discounted" assets like FLP interests or minority stock in a closely held business to provide for an increase or decrease in the dollars paid to the income beneficiaries, adjusting the payout to the stated percentage of the value as finally determined for gift tax purposes.

3. The regulations spell out precisely how the income and remainder interests are to be calculated for all split income trusts.

Reg Sec. 25.7520-1 states in part:

(b) COMPONENTS OF VALUATION —

    (1) INTEREST RATE COMPONENT —

        (i) SECTION 7520 INTEREST RATE. The section 7520 interest rate is the rate of return, rounded to the nearest two-tenths of one percent, that is equal to 120 percent of the applicable Federal mid-term rate, compounded annually, for purposes of section 1274(d)(1), for the month in which the valuation date falls. In rounding the rate to the nearest two-tenths of a percent, any rate that is midway between one two-tenths of a percent and another is rounded up to the higher of those two rates. For example, if 120 percent of the applicable Federal mid-term rate is 10.30, the section 7520 interest rate component is 10.4. The section 7520 interest rate is published monthly by the Internal Revenue Service in the Internal Revenue Bulletin (See section 601.601 (d)(2)(ii)(b) of this chapter).

        (ii) VALUATION DATE. Generally, the valuation date is the date on which the gift is made. For gift tax purposes, the valuation date is the date on which the gift is complete under section 25.2511-2. For special rules in the case of charitable transfers, see section 25.7520-2.

    (2) MORTALITY COMPONENT. The mortality component reflects the mortality data most recently available from the United States

census. As new mortality data becomes available after each de-
cennial census, the mortality component described in this section
will be revised periodically and the revised mortality component
tables will be published in the regulations at that time. For gifts
with valuation dates after April 30, 1989, the mortality component table (Table 80CNSMT) is contained in section 20.2031-
7(d) of this chapter (Estate Tax Regulations). See section 20.
2031-7A of this chapter for mortality component tables applicable to gifts before May 1, 1989.

(c) TABLES. The present value on the valuation date of an annuity, life
state, term of years, remainder, or reversion is computed by using the section 7520 interest rate component that is described in paragraph (b)(1) of
this section and the mortality component that is described in paragraph
(b)(2) of this section. Actuarial factors for determining these present values are included in tables in these regulations and in publications by the
Internal Revenue Service. If a special factor is required in order to value an
interest, the Internal Revenue Service will furnish the factor upon a request for a ruling. The request for a ruling must be accompanied by a recitation of the facts, including the date of birth for each measuring life and
copies of relevant instruments. A request for a ruling must comply with the
instructions for requesting a ruling published periodically in the Internal
Revenue Bulletin (see Rev. Proc. 94-1, 1994-1

I.R.B. 10, and subsequent updates, and sections 601.201 and
601.601(d)(2)(ii)(b) of this chapter) and include payment of the required
user fee.

Chapter 15

1. In 1990 there were a number of changes revolving around transfers to
   heirs which included interests in the property retained by the grantors.
   IRC§2702 specifically provides for the qualified personal residence
   trust.
2. The following Private Letter Ruling (9626041) issued in April, 1996
   provides an excellent technical overview of the QPRT, including the
   ability of the grantors to lease the house after the term of the qualified
   residence interest in the trust.

   This is in response to your letter dated November 22, 1995, and
   other submissions in which you request rulings that the proposed
   trusts, holding property as described below, will be qualified personal
   residence trusts (QPRTs) satisfying the requirements of section 25.
   2702-5(c) of the Gift Tax Regulations, and that the property placed in
   the trusts will not be includible in each taxpayers' gross estate if the
   taxpayer survives the term of the trust.

   You represent that taxpayer A and taxpayer B are married. Each
   taxpayer proposes to create an irrevocable trust and transfer his or her
   undivided 50 percent tenancy in common interest in their residential
   property to the trust. The terms of the proposed trusts are intended to

satisfy the requirements for qualified personal residence trusts in section 25.2702-5(c).

The residential property that taxpayer A and taxpayer B propose to transfer to the trusts, is equivalent or smaller in size to the other residential properties in the area. The taxpayers use the property primarily as their personal residence.

Under each proposed trust agreement, the taxpayer creating that trust will be entitled to the use and occupancy of the residence for a fifteen-year term. At the end of the fifteen-year term, the trust will continue and the residence will remain in the trust. The beneficial ownership of the property held in each trust will, however, pass to the taxpayers' children or their issue. The terms of each trust permit the taxpayer of that trust to lease the property from the trust at its fair market value rent. The trust will terminate at the earlier of the death of the taxpayer or a time agreed upon by the taxpayer and the beneficial owners of the property.

If a taxpayer dies prior to the expiration of the fifteen-year term, the property held by that taxpayer's trust is to pass to his or her estate. Each taxpayer has prepared a will which provides that, if the taxpayer/decedent's interest in the residential property is included in the taxpayer's gross estate, the interest in the residential property will pass outright to the surviving spouse.

With respect to the trust created by taxpayer A, if, for any reason, the residence ceases to be held as taxpayer A's personal residence during the retained term and prior to his death, his trust will either terminate and all assets will be distributed to taxpayer A, or the trustee may, within 30 days, convert the personal residence trust into a qualified annuity trust as described in section 25.2702-3(b). The amount of the annuity to be paid to taxpayer A at least annually after the conversion may not be less than an amount determined under section 25.2702-5(c)(8)(ii)(C). The trust created by taxpayer B has similar terms.

You request that we rule as follows:

1. The property to be transferred by taxpayer A and taxpayer B to the proposed trusts is a personal residence within the meaning of section 25.2702-5(c)(2).

2. The proposed trusts will be qualified personal residence trusts within the meaning of section 25.2702-5(c).

3. If either or both of the taxpayers survive the 15-year term of their trust and continue to live in the residence leasing the residence for fair market value rent, the interest in the property that each taxpayer transfers to his or her trust will not be includible in that taxpayer's gross estate under section 2036.

ISSUES 1 and 2 (QUALIFIED PERSONAL RESIDENCE TRUST)

Section 2702(a) provides special valuation rules for determining the value of a transfer for gift tax purposes where a donor transfers property in trust to or for the benefit of a member of the donor's family, and the donor retains an interest in the trust. Section 2702(a)(3)(A)(ii) provides that section 2702 shall not apply to a transfer if it involves the transfer of an interest in trust, all the property of which consists of a residence to be used as a personal residence by persons holding term interests in the trust (i.e., a personal residence trust).

Section 25.2702-5(a) provides, in part, that a qualified personal residence trust as defined in section 25.2702-5(c) is treated as a personal residence trust satisfying the requirements of section 2702(a)(3) (A)(ii). Section 25.2702-5(c) provides that the requirements for a qualified personal residence trust must be satisfied in provisions in the governing instrument and these provisions by their terms must continue in effect during any term interest in the trust.

Section 25.2702-5(c)(2)(i) provides that a personal residence of a term holder is either, the principle residence of the term holder (within the meaning of section 1034), one other residence of the term holder (within the meaning of section 280A(d)(1) but without regard to section 280A(d)(2)), or an undivided fractional interest in either. A personal residence may include appurtenant structures used by the term holder for residential purposes and adjacent land not in excess of that which is reasonably appropriate for residential purposes (taking into account the residence's size and location).

In the present case, the terms of the proposed trusts satisfy the requirements for qualified personal residence trusts as set forth in section 25.2702-5(c). The property to be transferred is an undivided fractional interest in the principle residence of taxpayer A and taxpayer B. The size of the property is reasonably appropriate for residential purposes taking into account the residence's size and location.

We conclude that the property to be transferred by taxpayer A and taxpayer B to the proposed trusts is a personal residence within the meaning of section 25.2702-5(c). In addition, we conclude that the proposed trusts will be qualified personal residence trusts within the meaning of section 25.2702-5(c).

ISSUE 3 (INCLUDIBILITY IN GROSS ESTATE)

Section 2033 provides that the gross estate shall include the value of all property in which the decedent has an interest at the time of his death.

Section 2036(a) provides that the value of the gross estate shall include the value of any property of which the decedent has made a transfer (except in the case of a bona fide sale for an adequate and full consideration in money or money's worth) in which the decedent has retained for his life the possession or enjoyment of, or the right to the income from the property, or the right to designate the persons who shall possess or enjoy the property or the income from the property.

In Estate of McNichol v. Commissioner, 265 F.2d 667 (3rd Cir. 1959), cert. den. 361 U.S. 829 (1960), the court held that "enjoyment" as used in the death tax statute is not a term of art, but is synonymous with substantial present economic benefit. In McNichol, the decedent purportedly conveyed income-producing real estate to his children 9 years before his death. Pursuant to an oral understanding with his children, the decedent continued to receive the rents from the properties until his death. The court held that the properties were includible in his gross estate under the predecessor to section 2036.

In Estate of Barlow v. Commissioner, 55 T.C. 666 (1971), acq., 1972-2 C.B. 1, the court held that, if a lessee/decedent is obligated to pay fair market rent from the date that the lessee transferred the property to the lessor, the decedent did not retain, for purposes of section 2036, possession or the enjoyment of, or the right to the income from the property if the decedent did not make the rental payments for a period of time prior to his death. The decedent and his spouse transferred a farm to their children and contemporaneously leased the property from the children at fair market value rent. The decedent and his spouse were legally obligated as tenants to pay this rent and the children were entitled, as landlords, to terminate the lease and oust the decedent and his spouse from the property if the rent was not paid. Although the decedent paid the rent for the first two years, the family agreed that, because of certain medical problems, the decedent need not continue to pay the rent, and the decedent did not pay the rent until his death four years later. Because the decedent was obligated to pay fair market value rent from the date of the transfer and there was no express or implied agreement at the date of the transfer that the decedent could avoid this rent obligation, the court held that the property was not includible in the decedent's gross estate under section 2036.

Rev. Rul. 70-155, 1970-1 C.B. 189, holds that a donor's continued occupancy of a transferred residence rent free until his death is as much an economic benefit as if he had rented the property and obtained the income therefrom.

In the present case, taxpayer A and taxpayer B each propose to transfer an undivided interest in their residential property to separate irrevocable trusts. At the termination of the initial 15-year term, the property will remain in trust (if the taxpayer survives) and A and B will have the option of leasing the property at its fair market value rent from their respective trusts. Because the property will be leased at fair market value rental, A and B will not receive an economic benefit from the property. Thus, A's and B's retained economic enjoyment of the property will cease when they begin paying the rental.

Under the terms of A's trust, if taxpayer A dies prior to the expiration of the 15-year term, the property held by his QPRT is to pass to his estate. The property would, thus, be includible in his gross estate under section 2033. You represent that taxpayer A has executed a will that devises any interest in the residence that may be includible in his gross estate, outright to taxpayer B, if she survives. Accordingly, if taxpayer A dies during the term of the QPRT, taxpayer B will own outright an undivided interest in the residential property. If taxpayer B then survives the term of her QPRT and leases the one-half interest in the property that she had transferred to this QPRT for fair market value rent, only the one-half interest that she holds outright will be includible in her gross estate if she owns and lives in the property at her death. This portion will be includible under section 2033.

Taxpayer B's trust and will contain similar provisions. Thus, if taxpayer B dies during the term of the QPRT, an undivided interest in the property will pass outright to taxpayer A. If A leases the one-half interest in the property that he had transferred to his QPRT for fair market value rent, only the one-half interest that he holds outright will be includible in his gross estate if he owns and lives in the property at his death.

We conclude that, if either or both of the taxpayers survive the 15-year term of their trust and continue to live in the residence leasing the residence for fair market value rent, the interest in the property that each taxpayer transfers to his or her trust will not be includible in that taxpayer's gross estate under section 2036.

Except as we have specifically ruled herein, we express no opinion under the cited provisions or under any other provision of the Code.

This ruling is based on the facts and applicable law in effect on the date of this letter. If there is a change in material fact or law (local or Federal) before the transactions considered in the ruling take effect, the ruling will have no force or effect. If the taxpayer is in doubt whether there has been a change in material fact or law, a request for reconsideration of this ruling should be submitted to this office.

This ruling is directed only to the taxpayer who requested it. Section 6110(j)(3) provides that it may not be used or cited as precedent.

3. The reason for the inclusion in the estate has nothing to do with the QPRT rules, per se, but instead to the all-encompassing nature of IRC§ 2036(a). This section causes inclusion of an assets transferred in which the grantor retains a life interest. If the grantor dies during the term of the trust, he will have de facto retained a life interest.

4. The children can gain deferral in two ways. Once the house becomes theirs and the parents pay rent, the house would be classified as rental property eligible for tax-deferred exchange under IRC§ 1031. If, after the parents moved from the house or died it was owned by one child, that child could convert it to a personal residence eligible for the capital gains exemption provided by IRC§ 121 .

5. It may seem counterintuitive, but the income tax provisions and the estate tax provisions of the Internal Revenue Code are not interrelated. There is no "grantor trust" concept in the estate tax chapters of the code that provide for inclusion in the estate just because the trust is a grantor trust for income tax purposes. In essence, if the grantor does not retain an interest in the trust that would cause him or her to be deemed the owner at death, the trust assets will not be included in the estate of the grantor.

Chapter 16

1. There will be a difference between "real" value and fair market value when an FLP interest is the asset in the trust. Tax is always imposed on fair market value. The important thing in this example is that GSTT is imposed at the end of the trust term. In the case of the Jackie O. Lead Trust some authorities have estimated that the value might be well in excess of $200 million at the end of the 24 year term, with 55 percent going to the government.

Chapter 17

1. Paul L. Comstock, *Financial Parenting Through a Family Foundation, Tusts and Estates.* August, 1992. Pg.32.
2. Private foundations are exempt from tax under §501(c)(3) which states in part:

Corporations, and any community chest, fund, or foundation, organized and operated exclusively for religious, charitable, scientific, testing for public safety, literary, or educational purposes, or to foster national or international amateur sports competition (but only if no part of its activities involve the provision of athletic facilities or equipment), or for the prevention of cruelty to children or animals, no part of the net earnings of which inures to the benefit of any private shareholder or individual, A private foundation is further described by exclusion is §509(a) which states:

(a) GENERAL RULE

For purposes of this title, the term "private foundation" means a domestic or foreign organization described in section 501(c)(3) **other than —**

(1) an organization described in section 170(b)(1)(A) (other than in clauses (vii) and (viii));

(2) an organization which —

    (A) normally receives more than one-third of its support in each taxable year from any combination of —

        (i) gifts, grants, contributions, or membership fees, and

        (ii) gross receipts from admissions, sales of merchandise, performance of services, or furnishing of facilities, in an activity which is not an unrelated trade or business (within the meaning of section 513), not including such receipts from any person, or from any bureau or similar agency of a governmental unit (as described in section 170(c)(1)), in any taxable year to the extent such receipts exceed the greater of $5,000 or 1 percent of the organization's support in such taxable year, from persons other than disqualified persons (as defined in section 4946) with respect to the organization, from governmental units described in section 170(c)(1), or from organizations described in section 170(b)(1)(A) (other than in clauses (vii) and (viii)).

3. The excise tax is detailed in IRC§4940(a). Net investment income is defined in IRC§4940(c).

4. SECTION 4946. DEFINITIONS AND SPECIAL RULES

(a) DISQUALIFIED PERSON

    (1) IN GENERAL

For purposes of this subchapter, the term "disqualified person" means, with respect to a private foundation, a person who is —

    (A) a substantial contributor to the foundation,

    (B) a foundation manager (within the meaning of subsection (b)(1)),

    (C) an owner of more than 20 percent of —

        (i) the total combined voting power of a corporation,

        (ii) the profits interest of a partnership, or

        (iii) the beneficial interest of a trust or unincorporated enterprise, which is a substantial contributor to the foundation,

    (D) a member of the family (as defined in subsection (d)) of any individual described in subparagraph (A), (B), or (C),

    (E) a corporation of which persons described in subparagraph (A), (B), (C), or (D) own more than 35 percent of the total combined voting power,

    (F) a partnership in which persons described in subparagraph (A), (B), (C), or (D) own more than 35 percent of the profits interest,

    (G) a trust or estate in which persons described in subparagraph (A), (B), (C), or (D) hold more than 35 percent of the beneficial interest,

    (H) only for purposes of section 4943, a private foundation —

        (i) which is effectively controlled (directly or indirectly) by the same person or persons who control the private foundation in question, or

        (ii) substantially all of the contributions to which were made (directly or indirectly) by the same person or persons described in subparagraph (A), (B), or (C), or members of their families (within the meaning of subsection (d)), who made (directly or indirectly) substantially all of the contributions to the private foundation in question, and

    (I) only for purposes of section 4941, a government official (as defined in subsection (c)).

    (2) SUBSTANTIAL CONTRIBUTORS

For purposes of paragraph (1), the term "substantial contributor" means a person who is described in section 507(d)(2).

    (3) STOCKHOLDINGS

For purposes of paragraphs (1)(C)(i) and (1)(E), there shall be taken into account indirect stockholdings which would be taken into account under section 267(c), except that, for purposes of this paragraph, section 267(c)(4) shall be treated as providing that the members of the family of an individual are the members within the meaning of subsection (d).

(4) PARTNERSHIPS; TRUSTS

For purposes of paragraphs (1)(C)(ii) and (iii), (1)(F), and (1)(G), the ownership of profits or beneficial interests shall be determined in accordance with the rules for constructive ownership of stock provided in section 267(c) (other than paragraph (3) thereof), except that section 267(c)(4) shall be treated as providing that the members of the family of an individual are the members within the meaning of subsection (d).

(b) FOUNDATION MANAGER

For purposes of this subchapter, the term "foundation manager" means, with respect to any private foundation —

(1) an officer, director, or trustee of a foundation (or an individual having powers or responsibilities similar to those of officers, directors, or trustees of the foundation), and

(2) with respect to any act (or failure to act), the employees of the foundation having authority or responsibility with respect to such act (or failure to act).

(c) GOVERNMENT OFFICIAL

For purposes of subsection (a)(1)(I) and section 4941, the term "government official" means, with respect to an act of self-dealing described in section 4941, an individual who, at the time of such act, holds any of the following offices or positions (other than as a "special Government employee", as defined in section 202(a) of title 18, United States Code):

(1) an elective public office in the executive or legislative branch of the Government of the United States,

(2) an office in the executive or judicial branch of the Government of the United States, appointment to which was made by the President,

(3) a position in the executive, legislative, or judicial branch of the Government of the United States —

    (A) which is listed in schedule C of rule VI of the Civil Service Rules, or

    (B) the compensation for which is equal to or greater than the lowest rate of compensation prescribed for GS-16 of the General Schedule under section 5332 of title 5, United States Code,

(4) a position under the House of Representatives or the Senate of the United States held by an individual receiving gross compensation at an annual rate of $15,000 or more,

(5) an elective or appointive public office in the executive, legislative, or judicial branch of the government of a State, possession of the United States, or political subdivision or other area of any of

the foregoing, or of the District of Columbia, held by an individual receiving gross compensation at an annual rate of $20,000 or more, or

(6) a position as personal or executive assistant or secretary to any of the foregoing.

(d) MEMBERS OF FAMILY

For purposes of subsection (a)(1), the family of any individual shall include only his spouse, ancestors, children, grandchildren, great grandchildren, and the spouses of children, grandchildren, and great grandchildren.

5. Treacy, Gerald B., Jr. *Supporting Organizations* Tax Management Portfolio 871. 1996. This portfolio is one of the most complete studies of the supporting organization yet published. It is an essential reference for any professional who intends to have a solid working understanding of this important entrepreneurial philanthropy tool.

6. Treacy, *ibid.* Most entrepreneurial Sos will be what are know as "Type III" organizations which are formed "operated *in connection with* the supported public harity or charities." These Sos will be required to name specific organizations to be supported. However, a community foundation could be named and through its donor-advised fund program the family could support numerous other causes.

7. While the vast majority of donor advised funds are indeed at public charities (for the higher deductibility limits), they can also be set up by a private foundation. An interesting private letter ruling dealt with how a DAF is set up, and on its affect, if any, on the exempt organization. Ltr. Rul. 9412039 (PLR), issued 12/23/93 stated in part:

RATIONALE

Your first ruling request asks whether the creation and maintenance of a separate donor advised fund will affect your status as an organization described in section 501(c)(3) of the Code. M and N plan to donate certain assets of timberlands to you. You will be the owner in fee of the assets. A portion of the income from the sale of the assets will be directed to be placed in a newly created, donor advised fund named after M. This fund will consist of all assets contributed to you that are directed to be allocated to the fund and the income, profits, gains and other proceeds attributable to such assets. An Advisory Committee of the fund will make recommendations as to charitable distributions from the fund. Although the Advisory Committee will make recommendations, your Board of Directors has the power to disregard these recommendations. If the recommendations are disregarded, the matter can then be referred to an independent party who, having been vested with the powers of the board, will make a binding decision regarding the charitable distribution. Because your board consists of M and two other directors, the board has the ability to act independently from M. M will not have control over the fund. Rather, your board will have ultimate control over the assets and income of the fund. Therefore, there will be no material conditions or restrictions on the assets transferred by M to you. Thus, the fund should be treated as an integral part of you and not as a separate entity. The facts presented in your ruling request establish that you will continue to engage primarily in activities which accomplish exempt purposes, and no substantial part of your activities will be in furtherance of nonexempt purposes as required by section 1.501(c)(3)-1(c)(1). Because the fund will be held and administered by you in a manner consistent with your exempt purposes, we conclude that the establishment of the fund within you in the manner described will not deprive you of your status as an organization described in section 501(c)(3) of the Code.

8. The following specimen DAF Agreement, provided courtesy of Dan Rice & Associates, may help to bettr understand how a DAF operates:

THE DAFNAME
PHILANTHROPIC FUND
MEMORANDUM OF UNDERSTANDING

Made MONTH _____, 199___, between DONOR1 and DONOR2 ("Donors"), residing at ADDRESS, and CHARITY, a STATE nonprofit corporation with its principal offices at CHARITY ADDRESS.

1. Donors intend from time to time to make gifts to CHARITY to be held and administered under the following terms and conditions.

2. A fund will be established on the books of CHARITY to be known as THE DAFNAME PHILANTHROPIC FUND (the "Fund").

3. The Fund will include the gift made today and described on attached Exhibit A, such other property as from time to time may be transferred to CHARITY by the Donors, or the survivor of them, for inclusion in the Fund, such property as from time to time may be received by CHARITY from any other source and accepted by it for inclusion in the Fund, and all income and other proceeds from the foregoing property.

4. The Fund will be the property of CHARITY and held by it in its corporate capacity; it will not be deemed a trust fund held by it in a trustee capacity; and it may be commingled with other funds held by CHARITY for comparable purposes. CHARITY, in its corporate capacity, will have ultimate authority and control over all property in the Fund, including any income earned by the Fund.

5. The Fund may be used only for charitable, religious or educational purposes (or any combination of such purposes). Ten percent (10 percent) of each dollar of income and principal shall be withdrawn from the Fund on December 31 of each year to be used directly by CHARITY in its own programs and ninety percent (90 percent) shall be used for the support of charitable organizations which are exempt from taxation under Section 501(c)(3) of the Internal Revenue Code of 1986 (the "Code"), which are described in Code Section 170(b)(1)(A), clauses (i) through (vi), contributions to which are deductible for income, gift and estate tax purposes, and whose purposes are not inconsistent with those of CHARITY.

6. The Board of Directors of CHARITY shall designate distributions from the Fund of income and principal within the limitations provided for in Paragraph 5 above. The Board of Directors will consider several criteria in determining the amount and timing of such distributions, with special weight given to donor advisory requests. Other criteria include recommendations from the Board and independent investigation by CHARITY staff evaluating the donor advisory requests to ensure that they are consistent with the needs and programs most deserving of support by CHARITY. Requests for distribution may be made by the Donors (and the survivor of them) and, following the death of the survivor of the Donors, by the Donors' children, from time to time, orally or in writing.

   Notwithstanding the foregoing, it is agreed and understood that: (a) the final discretion as to the use of the Fund income and principal shall be that of CHARITY's Board of Directors; (b) at least the income thereof will be withdrawn annually from the Fund; and (c) any income and principal remaining in the Fund at the death of the surviving Donor's child may be withdrawn in the sole discretion of CHARITY and used for its general purposes.

7. It is intended that the Fund be an integral part of CHARITY and not a separate trust. Nothing in this memorandum of understanding shall affect the status of CHARITY as an organization described in Code Section 501(c)(3) and as an organization which is not a private foundation within the meaning of Code Section 509(a). It is the express intention of CHARITY that the Fund be organized and operated to comply with Treasury Regulations Section 1.170(a)-9(e)(10-13). Nevertheless, both CHARITY and the Donors recognize that gifts from the Fund to other organizations may be treated as direct gifts from the Donors. This memorandum shall be interpreted in a manner consistent with the foregoing intention and so as to conform to the requirements of the foregoing provisions of the federal tax laws and any regulations issued pursuant thereto. CHARITY is authorized to amend this memorandum to conform to the provisions of any applicable law or government regulation in order to carry out the foregoing intention. References herein to provisions of the Internal Revenue Code of 1986 shall be deemed references to the corresponding provisions of any future Internal Revenue law.

Index